Ways of the Six-Footed

Ways of the Six-Footed

by ANNA BOTSFORD COMSTOCK

A reissue of the 1903 edition
with a new Foreword by
EDWARD H. SMITH

Cornell University Press

ITHACA AND LONDON

First published 1903 by Ginn & Company, Boston
Reissued 1977 with Foreword by Edward H. Smith

International Standard Book Number 0-8014-1081-9
Library of Congress Catalog Card Number 76-56639
Printed in the United States of America by Vail-Ballou Press, Inc.
Librarians: Library of Congress cataloging information appears on the last page of the book.

TO

ALL THOSE WHO HAVE BEEN MY GOOD COMRADES AND
FELLOW LOITERERS IN NATURE'S BYWAYS
THIS BOOK IS DEDICATED

ILLUSTRATIONS BY
>*W. C. BAKER AND*
>*O. L. FOSTER, AND*
>*THE AUTHOR*

FOREWORD, 1977

Anna Botsford Comstock's book for children was first published over seventy years ago, but it retains its original appeal for nature lovers of all ages. The author's accounts of insect life are still accurate today, and convey her joy in the beauty of nature and her fascination with living things in their natural habitat. She sees the insects competing for survival in an orderly but complex world.

In this delightful little volume Mrs. Comstock has selected some common species to illustrate the remarkable adaptability of insects. Her subjects include ants, bees, wasps, butterflies, crickets, cicadas, and lace wings. These stories illustrate the social organization of insects, their communication by sound, their employment of mimicry as a defense strategy, migration, and other adaptive features. Her reports are filled with detailed knowledge derived from careful observations and enlivened by her ability as a storyteller and by her enthusiasm for the setting in which her observations are made.

Anna Botsford became a student at Cornell in 1874, six years after its founding. She had been reared in

Cattaraugus County, New York, and she brought to her college experience a deep love for the natural world. This had been cultivated by her mother, who delighted in field trips for nature study with her daughter.

Anna Botsford's arrival at Cornell coincided with an exciting stage of discovery and development in the natural history disciplines. She enrolled in a course offered by John Henry Comstock, a promising young entomologist. In 1878 they were married and began a partnership that, in the more than fifty years that followed, contributed to the study of entomology and nature at Cornell.

Together the Comstocks published fourteen books. Mrs. Comstock contributed as author, teacher, and artist. She became one of the foremost wood engravers of her time, and her skill in this art is perhaps best seen in her illustrations for *An Introduction to Entomology,* the comprehensive volume by her husband. Her own best-known book, *Handbook of Nature Study,* was first published in 1911 and has appeared in twenty-four editions. It is still regarded as a classic in its field.

Cornell University enlisted Mrs. Comstock's special teaching skills when the agricultural reverses of the 1890s caused many young people to leave the farms for the cities, where they were ill prepared to compete.

Mrs. Comstock's assignment was to organize and implement a program that would place farm life in a more appealing light and thereby stem the exodus. She believed that nature study for schoolchildren could be a primary means to this end. Her objective was to share her experience with parents and teachers and enable them to transmit an appreciation of nature. Her sympathies with the teacher are well illustrated in the introduction to *Handbook of Nature Study*. Here she encourages parents and teachers to draw on commonplace events of natural history to develop the children's understanding of living systems and a view of life and death as natural events.

Mrs. Comstock was accorded many honors during her lifetime. She was the first woman appointed to the faculty at Cornell and an early member of Sigma Xi, a national honorary research society that was founded at Cornell. In 1923 she was named one of America's twelve greatest women by the League of Women Voters. In 1930, Hobart College awarded her the honorary degree of Doctor of Humane Letters.

The decade of the 1970s has witnessed a remarkable growth in ecological awareness. From our reassessments of the quality of life has come the realization that technological advances do not replace our need for kinship with the natural world, or for common interests shared by parent and child. In the context of this rediscovered wisdom new readers can share the author's ''sense of the dignity and grandeur of this great silent struggle for adjustment and supremacy.''

EDWARD H. SMITH

ITHACA, NEW YORK

PREFACE

THE stories in this volume were written with the definite purpose of illustrating the great primal truth that wherever there is life there are problems confronting it; and that the way of solving these problems has been the way to success in the evolution of a species. The writer has hoped to depict also, in some measure, the dignity of life's upward struggle, however humble the incarnation.

No excuse is offered that the facts herein given were not ascertained through original and personal investigations; the object of the volume is not to give new facts, but rather to give another standpoint for viewing the facts already known. Yet the reason for selecting these particular stories out of a world full is that I have read chapters of them with mine own eyes, and have been able here and there to add something not before recorded. The complete story of the *Ceratina* was brought to me page by page from the fields by my husband for my daily entertainment while I was prostrated by a tedious illness. The Little Nomad was my special chum during a summer vacation. The Seine Maker is a water sprite that has lured me to various indiscreet excursions to the middle of swift streams. And the crickets, bees, wasps, and ants have been our boon companions for many a happy summer and autumn.

" The Story we love Best " was published in the *Saint Nicholas* magazine in June, 1889. " The Perfect Socialism," " Pipers and Minnesingers," and portions of " Two Mother Masons " and " A Sheep in Wolf's Clothing " were printed in different numbers of the *Chautauquan* during the year 1898. " A Tactful Mother " and " A Dweller in Tents " were written for the young readers of the *Observer* in 1897, and " Hermit and Troubadour " appeared in the *Cornell Nature-study Bulletin* for June, 1899.

I wish to acknowledge the courtesy of The Century Co., of Dr. Theodore L. Flood, of Dr. Edward F. Bigelow, and of the Cornell University Nature-study Bureau for cordial permission to reprint these several stories. I also wish to acknowledge the helpfulness of Mr. W. C. Baker and Mr. O. L. Foster in obtaining for me suitable illustrations. And I wish to express my thanks to Miss Mary C. Dickerson for the use of Figs. 21 and 26, and to Miss Mary E. King, whose direct assistance has enabled me to prepare this volume for publication at the present time.

ANNA BOTSFORD COMSTOCK.

ITHACA, N.Y., April, 1903.

CONTENTS

CHAPTER		PAGE
I.	PIPERS AND MINNESINGERS	3
II.	A LITTLE NOMAD	29
III.	A SHEEP IN WOLF'S CLOTHING	39
IV.	THE PERFECT SOCIALISM	55
V.	TWO MOTHER MASONS	96
VI.	THE STORY WE LOVE BEST	108
VII.	A DWELLER IN TENTS	119
VIII.	A TACTFUL MOTHER	125
IX.	A SEINE MAKER	133
X.	HERMIT AND TROUBADOUR	140

ILLUSTRATIONS

PAGE

A Country Highway that leads past Wood and Orchard. By O. L.
Foster 2

Antenna of Male Mosquito 8

The Lyreman. An Arboreal Wooer 11

Meadow Grasshopper 17

Wing-cover of Male Meadow Grasshopper. Showing Musical
Organ 18

Wing-cover of Female Meadow Grasshopper. Not a Musical
Instrument 18

A Katydid 19

Musical Instrument of the Katydid 20

Ear of Katydid 20

Wing-cover of Male Cricket 22

When the Afternoon Shadows in the Orchard lengthen. By W. C.
Baker 23

Ear of Cricket 24

Snowy Tree-cricket 25

A Restful, Woodsy Path. By O. L. Foster 28

Twin Maples. By W. C. Baker 31

Maple-leaf Cutter. Moth and Camping-ground of Caterpillar . 32

Caterpillar of Maple-leaf Cutter enlarged 33

Tent Ropes of the Maple-leaf Cutter. Camera Lucida Sketch . 34

A Lilliputian Mud-turtle 36

The Home of the Young Viceroy. By W. C. Baker . . . 40

PAGE

A. Young Viceroy Caterpillar. *B.* Winter Home of Viceroy Caterpillar. By Mary C. Dickerson 42

"So humpy and spiny that no bird would touch him" . . . 44

"An uneven morsel". 45

The Viceroy 47

The Monarch 48

"Smug-looking Caterpillars." By Mary C. Dickerson . . . 50

Olden Cities. By W. C. Baker 54

An Ant Town. By W. C. Baker 63

An Ant Cow-shed. By M. V. Slingerland 77

The Dwelling of a Wasp Commune. By W. C. Baker . . . 81

Neighborly Communes. By O. L. Foster 87

Some Bush or Tree near a Stream. By W. C. Baker . . . 95

"A fidgety being" 97

The Jug Builder and her Nests 102

"A raspberry bramble, low trailing, and graceful." By W. C.
Baker 107

Little Carpenter Bee and her Nest 111

A Basswood Tree. By W. C. Baker 118

A Basswood Leaf rolled into Tents 120

The Tent-dweller 121

Head and Two Thoracic Segments of Caterpillar of *P. limata* . 123

Moth of the Basswood Leaf-roller 124

Lace-wing Fly and her Eggs, Larva, and Cocoon 127

The Haunts of the "Water-sprite." By O. L. Foster . . . 132

A Seine and the Fisherman's Hut 134

The Wider Levels. By O. L. Foster 135

The Home Tree of Little Hermit Brother. By W. C. Baker . . 139

"Good-by now to cowl and robe" 146

Ways of the Six-Footed

Fig. 1. A Country Highway that leads past Wood and Orchard.

WAYS OF THE SIX-FOOTED

I

PIPERS AND MINNESINGERS

E are wont to speak of "the silence of the night" or "the silence of the woods and fields." We find such silence restful and soothing when we are weary of the din of cities and the noise of crowded thoroughfares. Yet if the listener in the summer meadows or summer darkness be analytic, if his ear be attuned to the harmonies of nature, he will discover that the air is filled with the soft music of a vast orchestra — music so continuous and so monotonous that it seems rather to belong to earth's silences than to earth's sounds. Few of us realize how oppressive would be utter silence; and few of us comprehend the debt of gratitude that we owe to

the little fiddlers in the grass, the drummers in the
trees, and the pipers in the air.   There is cheer in
their music, as well as restfulness.   Their fugues
afford companionship, and at the same time inspire
in us a comfortable sense of isolation and peace.

The subject of insect music should not be dealt
with as a purely scientific study, for it has been
closely connected with the poetry of the ages. A discussion of these little musicians would be incomplete
without reference to the impression they have made
upon the poet mind, which ever reflects, intensified,
the experiences of humanity.   Among those poets
who really take us into the fields some have paid
tribute to our insect friends.   But among the vast
hordes of insects only a few have been chosen as fit
subjects for song.   These favored ones are butterflies,
moths, flies, bees, fireflies, dragonflies, cicadas, grasshoppers, crickets, katydids, and beetles.   Of these
twelve kinds of insects it will be noticed seven are
musicians, and are almost invariably mentioned in
connection with the sounds they make, as "the
buzzing fly," "the droning bee."   All this proves
that our literary people are better at listening than
at seeing; for to the naturalist there are many other
insects that press more deeply into the realm of poetry
than do these.

It is true that the great majority of our species of insects are silent. The few insects which make sounds do not have true voices. As insects do not breathe through their mouths, but through holes arranged along each side of the body, they naturally possess no such arrangement for vocalization connected with breathing as we find in our larynx.

The sounds made by insects may be divided into three classes: first, sounds emitted to frighten the foe; second, sounds made in connection with flight; and third, true love songs. The insects making sounds of the first sort are few; they make clicking or grating noises and clearly do not belong to the musical tribes.

The buzzing and droning notes given off by insects when flying may be accidental or may be of some significance to the insects; we really know very little of the methods or reasons for these songs. When we hear a certain buzzing we are just as sure that a fly has been caught in a spider's web as we are after we see the remonstrating little victim. But, whether or not this noise is of any use to the fly, we do not know. Those of us who have had experience with bees know very well by their buzzing whether they are happy, distressed, or angry; we know, too, that they are well aware of each other's emotions;

but whether they gain their intelligence through hearing different sounds, as we do, is a matter not yet settled. We know, however, that the piping of a young queen in her cell, just before a second swarm emerges, excites the whole colony greatly; thus we have evidence that bees are sensitive to at least one sound.

The older naturalists made futile experiments to discover whether the sounds of the bees and flies were involuntary and caused simply by the vibrations of the air made by rapid motions of the wings; or if the note given off was caused by air expelled from the spiracles against the vibrating wings, on the same plan as the note of the jews'-harp. Recent investigations seem to show that the vibration of the walls of the thorax, as well as the vibrations of the wings, cause the sound. As for myself, I prefer to believe that the mellow hum which pervades the air of midsummer afternoons is a voluntary hymn of praise for sunshine and blue skies.

THE PIPERS

The poets have not been generally complimentary to flies. Tennyson, in one of the most bitter stanzas of "Maud," says : —

> "Far off from the clamor of liars belied in the
> hubbub of lies
>
>   *   *   *   *   *   *

Where each man walks with his head in a cloud
of poisonous flies."

Shakespeare alludes to them several times in much
the same spirit.

Of all the members of the families of flies, the
mosquito has received most personal attention from
the poets; perhaps because she has been lavish in
personal attentions to them. Bryant has deemed her
worthy of a separate poem, in which he recognizes
her as a fellow-singer : —

"Thou'rt welcome to the town; but why come here
To bleed a brother poet, gaunt like thee ?
Alas, the little blood I have is dear,
And thin will be the banquet drawn from me."

How much we might enjoy the song of the mosquito
if it were not associated with the unwilling yielding
of blood to the singer is problematical. Perhaps if
Beethoven's Pastoral Symphony were always to be
played in our hearing when we were occupying the
dentist's chair, we would soon become averse to its
exquisite harmonies. Therefore it is no wonder that
we do not think of music at all when we hear the
distant horn of the mosquito; instead, we listen with
patient exasperation as the sound grows louder, and
we wait nervously for the final sharp " zzzzz " which
announces that the audacious singer has selected a

place upon us which she judges will be a good site
for a pumping station. We do not like her noise a
whit better even though it be a love song.

The mosquito is an exception to all other insect minnesingers, for she is the only one among them all that
belongs to the female sex. The lover for whom she
sings is a quiet, gentlemanly fellow who never troubles
us, as he has no taste for blood ; he may be found upon
the window-panes, and may be recognized by his
feathery antennæ, which stand out in front of his head
like a pair of pompons. The physicist, Professor A. M.

FIG. 2.

Antenna of
Male Mosquito.

Mayer, performed some interesting experiments which seem to prove beyond doubt
that the antennæ of the male mosquito
are organs of hearing. Figure 2 shows
one of these antennæ. It will be noted
that each segment bears a whorl of hairs
and that these whorls diminish in size
toward the tip of the antenna. The
experiment was as follows : Professor Mayer cemented
a mosquito to a glass slide without injuring him, and
observed him through a microscope while an assistant
sounded tuning forks, varying in pitch, in different
parts of the room. The note from a fork of low pitch
caused the basal whorl of hairs to vibrate ; a note from
a higher key caused a whorl of hairs nearer the tip to

vibrate. Thus Professor Mayer found that the range of one of these antennæ extended over the middle and next higher octaves of a piano. From this it seems that this insect is equipped to enjoy the music of his lady; not only this, but, as was shown by further experiments, he is enabled to tell in what direction to find her. The large globular basal segment of the antenna has been found, on dissection, to be an auditory capsule.

If poets have found little to enjoy in the buzzing of flies, they have been most appreciative of the other wing-singers, the bees; the allusions to their soothing strains are innumerable. The song of

> " The golden banded bees
> Droning o'er the flowery leas "

seems to have been comforting and dear to humanity for many centuries. The poetic literature devoted to bees is much larger than that given to any other insect, and at the same time more casual. They are constantly alluded to as companions of the flowers, and are, in the poet mind, an essential part of bloom-decked meadows and hillsides. Their peaceful hum is the background against which clover and fruit blooms are painted.

> " The blossomed apple tree,
> Among its flowery tufts, on every spray,

> Offers the wandering bee
> A fragrant chapel for his matin lay."

Thus Bryant finds the bee a " Fellow Worshipper."

The bumblebee has ever been a favorite with American poets. Emerson has thought her worthy a separate poem, in which he pays this tribute to her music : —

> " Hot midsummer's petted crone,
> Sweet to me thy drowsy tone
> Tells of countless sunny hours,
> Long days, and solid banks of flowers."

THE MINNESINGERS

To the minnesingers belong the insects which sing in order to facilitate their wooings. These are all of the masculine gender and are provided by nature with various sorts of instruments, upon which they play for the delectation of their ladies, who are mostly shy, silent creatures ; however, they seem to have a very appreciative and, at the same time, a very discriminating taste for music. The first of the insect troubadours which we will study is the cicada.

This musician is no near relative of the other love singers, as he belongs to another order of insects altogether. He is an interesting-looking fellow, with a stout body and broad, transparent wings quite ornately veined. Probably because of his song, his name has become confused with that of the locust, which is always a true grasshopper. The cicada whose song is the most familiar to us is the " dog-day harvest-fly " or " Lyreman " (Fig. 3). It resembles the seventeen-year species, except that it is larger and requires only two or three years in the immature state, below ground, instead of seventeen. The Lyreman when seen from above is black, with dull-green scroll ornamentation; below he is covered with white powder. He lives in trees; hidden beneath the leaves, this arboreal wooer sends forth a high trill, which seems to steep the senses of the listener in the essence of summer noons. If

Fig. 3. The Lyreman — an arboreal wooer.

you chance to find a Lyreman fallen from his perch and take him in your hand, he will sing and you can feel his body vibrate with the sound. But it will remain a mystery where the musical instrument is situated, for it is nowhere visible to the uninitiated. However, if you place him on his back, you may see directly behind the base of each hind leg a circular plate, nearly a quarter of an inch in diameter; beneath each of these

plates is a cavity across which is stretched a partition
made up of three distinct kinds of membranes for the
modulation of the tone; at the top of each cavity is a
stiff, folded membrane which acts as a drumhead; but
it is set in vibration by muscles instead of drumsticks,
and these muscles move so rapidly that we cannot distinguish the separate vibrations.   Thus, our Lyreman is
provided with a very complicated pair of kettledrums,
which he plays with so much skill that his music sounds
more like that of a mandolin than of a drum.

The cicada was regarded as almost divine by the
early Greeks.   When Homer wished to compliment his
best orators he compared them to cicadas.   Anacreon,
the most graceful of the lyric poets of Greece, addresses
him thus : —

> " Sweet prophet of summer, loved of the Muses,
>   Beloved of Phœbus who gave thee thy shrill song,
>   Old age does not wear upon thee;
>   Thou art earth-born, musical, impassive, without blood.
>   Thou art almost a god."

The Greeks were so much attached to these insects
that they kept them in cages for the sake of their
songs; they wore images of them in their hair.   The
song of the cicada was the name given to the sound of
the harp; a cicada upon a harp was the emblem of the
science of music.   We all know the beautiful story of

the rival musicians, Eunomus and Ariston, and how during a contest in harp-playing a cicada flew to the instrument of Eunomus, took the place of a broken string, and thus won for him the victory. The ancients also seem to have known something of the habits of these insects, for the cynical Xenarchus tells us : —

> " Happy the cicadas' lives
> Since they all have voiceless wives."

Virgil also pays tribute to the cicadas thus : —

> " Et cantu querulae rumpent arbusta Cicadae."

The English poets have also paid the cicadas some attention. Byron, who seldom mentions the smaller things in nature, writes : —

> " The shrill cicadas, people of the pine,
> Make their summer lives one ceaseless song."

The most graphic description of the song of our own cicada is given by Elizabeth Akers in the lines : —

> " The shy cicada, whose noon voice rings
> So piercing shrill that it almost stings
> The sense of hearing."

James Whitcomb Riley also characterizes him in his own vivid way in the poem on " The Beetle " : —

> " The shrilling locust slowly sheathes
> His dagger voice and creeps away
> Beneath the brooding leaves, where breathes
> The zephyr of the dying day."

Surely a new interest attaches to this summer-day song when we realize that it has pleased the human ear since the dim age of Homer. The cicada's kettledrums are perhaps the only musical instruments now in use that have remained unchanged through a thousand centuries since they were first mentioned.

The other of the insect love singers belong to the order Orthoptera and are quite closely related to each other. First among these are short-horned grass-hoppers, although they are not so musical as some of the other species. However, we find in this group some veritable fiddlers. The long hind leg which is roughened with short spines is used as a fiddle bow, and is drawn across the wing cover, which acts the part of the fiddle, and gives off certain notes. These are our common grasshoppers and may be watched while fid-dling if one has the patience and wariness. These insects have found many admirers among the poets. Leigh Hunt apostrophizes the grasshopper thus : —

> "Green little vaulter in the sunny grass
> Catching your heart up at the feel of June,
> Sole voice that's heard amid the lazy noon."

And Keats writes thus : —

> " The poetry of earth is never dead ;
> When all the birds are faint with the hot sun,
> And hide in cooling trees, a voice will run

> From hedge to hedge about the new-mown mead;
> That is the grasshopper's.   He takes the lead
>   In summer luxury."

As may be inferred from these allusions these grass-hoppers sing during the heat of the day.

Other species of this same group of grasshoppers make their music by rubbing the front surface of the hind wings against the under surface of the wing covers.   This can only be accomplished when the insect is flying.   The note is a crackling sound; however, it is no accidental noise; it is as true a song as any, as I am sure all observers will agree who have seen one of these great, brown, roadside grasshoppers fly up into the air and hold himself there poised for minutes while he performs in apparent ecstasy his rapid, monotonous *pizzicato*.   James Whitcomb Riley has seen him, as the following lines prove : —

> " Where the dusty highway leads,
>   High above the wayside weeds
>   They sowed the air with butterflies, like blooming
>   flower seeds,
>   Till the dull grasshopper sprung
>   Half a man's height up, and hung
>   Tranced in the heat with whirring wings and sung
>   and sung and sung."

This description is so accurate that it actually identifies the species.   Mr. Riley is the prince among

poets that have sung Nature's melodies in America.
His sensitiveness to all out-of-door life, and his keen
eyes, unto which not only the poetry but the truth of
the fields and woods are revealed, make him a special
delight to naturalists.   They have to make no mental
reservations when reading his poems.   Elizabeth Akers
was another satisfactory naturalist poet, and she too
has noted this roadside grasshopper.   She says : —

> " The flying grasshopper clacked his wings
> Like castanets gayly beating."

Correlated with love singing must also be love listening.   While many insects have the chordotonal or true
hearing organs inside the body, only a few have these
connected with what we would, at first sight, call ears ;
and it is interesting to note the odd places in which
these ears are situated.   The grasshoppers which have
been described have their ears placed on each side of
the body on the segment behind the one to which the
hind legs are attached.   These little ears may be seen
with the naked eye if the insect's wings be lifted out of
the way ; in appearance they are nearly circular disks.
The first thought is, " Of course, since these ears were
developed to hear love songs, they would naturally be
nearer the heart than our own."   Unfortunately for
this theory an insect's anatomy is not arranged like

ours. The insect heart is a tube that extends along the back, like our backbone, and it is a most disconcerting organ when regarded as a possible locality for sentiment.

The long-horned or meadow grasshoppers are usually bright green or pale brown in color and occur in the taller grass of the meadows. They have long antennæ, as delicate as fine silken threads, which they keep constantly in motion (Fig. 4). These musicians have an apparatus for singing quite different from that of their shorthorned cousins. The wingcovers, near their bases at

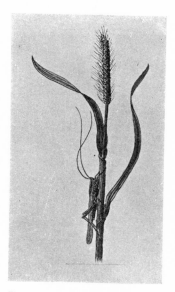

Fig. 4. Meadow Grasshopper.

the middle of the back, have a portion enlarged and sustained by strong veins (Fig. 5). One of these veins is ridged, and when drawn across the edge of the other wing-cover causes a vibration. The note given off is high but soft and pleasing; we associate it with the meadows in haying time and the heat of the day; however, several of our common species sing in the evening exclusively.   One species of these grasshoppers lives in trees.   The meadow grasshoppers have their ears in the same place as do the katydids (Fig. 9).

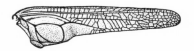

FIG. 5. Wing-cover of Male Meadow Grasshopper.   Showing Musical Organ.

FIG. 6.   Wing-cover of Female Meadow Grasshopper.   Not a Musical Instrument.

Another singer of love songs is the katydid.

> " I love to hear thine earnest voice
> Wherever thou art hid,
> Thou testy little dogmatist,
> Thou pretty katydid.
> Thou mindest me of gentle folks,
> Old gentle folks are they,
> Thou say'st an undisputed thing
> In such a solemn way."

I think this musician must have been some distance from Dr. Holmes when he wrote these lines; for distance is needful to lend enchantment to the katydid's song.   The grating emphasis of the assertion " Ka′-ty did ′, she did ′," is nerve-lacerating when the listener is in close proximity to this bass viol of the insect orchestra.   Mr. Riley describes the song well when he says : —

> " The katydid is rasping at
> The silence from the tangled broom."

The word "rasping" is peculiarly felicitous in this description; Elizabeth Akers used it also: —

> "The katydid with its rasping dry
> Made forever the same reply,
> Which laughing voices would still deny."

The katydids are near relatives to the meadow grass-hoppers; they live in trees and sing only in the evening and night. Despite his heavy voice the katydid is

Fig. 7. Katydid.

a very shy insect; the only sure way to find him is to take a lantern and, guided by the sound, discover his retreat while his attention is distracted by his quite distracting song. When found he is well worth looking at; he is dressed in pea-green; his wing-covers are so leaf-like in form and color that it is no wonder he is invisible when perched among the leaves. His face wears a very solemn expression, but somewhere in it is a suggestion of drollery, as if he could appreciate a joke; he keeps his long silken antennæ waving in an inquiring way that suggests curiosity rather than fear. Figure 7 is a picture of our common katydid; it shows the front triangular portion of the wing, which is the instrument with which the katydid plays. Figure 8 shows the details of the triangular bases of the upper wings from beneath; *l* is the left wing triangle and *r* is that of the right wing;

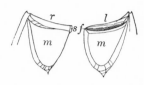

Fig. 8. Musical Instrument of the Katydid.

the left triangle bears the file (*f*) and the right triangle bears the scraper (*s*); in the central portion of each triangle is a translucent membrane (*m*), which is set into vibration when the scraper is drawn across the file and transmits the movement to the entire wing. The file is so large that it can be seen plainly with the naked eye. The song is so exactly like our own enunciation of the words "Katy did, Katy did, she did," that the singer seems almost uncanny, and attracts universal attention wherever he abounds.

Of the insect musicians the cricket is easily the most popular. Long associated with man, as a companion of the hearth and the field, his song touches ever the

Fig. 9. Ear of Katydid.

chords of human experience. Although we, in America, do not have the house-cricket which English poets

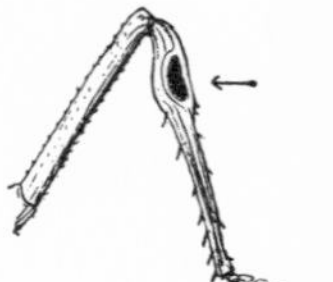

praise, yet our field-crickets have a liking for warm
corners, and will, if encouraged, take up their abode
among our hearthstones. The greatest tribute to the
music of the cricket is the wide range of human
emotion which it expresses. "As merry as a cricket"
is a very old saying and is evidence that the cricket's
fiddling has ever chimed with the gay moods of dancers
and merrymakers. Again, the cricket's song is made
an emblem of peace; and again we hear that the
cricket's "plaintive cry" is taken as the harbinger of
the sere and dying year. From happiness to utter
loneliness is the gamut covered by this sympathetic
song. Leigh Hunt found him glad and thus addresses
him : —

> "And you, warm little housekeeper who class
>   With those who think the candles come too soon,
> Loving the fire, and with your tricksome tune
>   Nick the glad, silent moments as they pass."

The chirp of the cricket is, in literature, usually
associated with the coming of autumn; but the careful
listener may hear him in the early summer, although
his song is not so insistent as later in the season. To
me it is the most enticing of all the insect strains; there
seems to be in it an invitation to "come and be cosy
and happy while the summer and the sunshine last." I
have also always been an admirer of the manly and self-

respecting methods of this little troubadour. He does
not wander abroad to seek his lady-love, but stands
sturdily at his own gate and plays his fiddle lustily,
always doing his best ; he knows the shy lady is not far
away, and that if she likes his song she will come to
him when her heart is won. It is very easy to see the
cricket making his " crink," as our British cousins call
his cry. If you are careful, you may observe him in
his own doorway ; or perhaps an easier method is to
catch several and place them in a glass jar in which
there is a little sod ; they will soon begin chirping in
such a cage and may be watched at leisure.

Each wing-cover of the male cricket is divided into
membranous, disklike spaces on top (Fig. 10), and across

each extends a vein covered with transverse
ridges, the " file " (f) ; on the inner edge,
near the base, is a hardened portion called
the " scraper " (s).   When chirping the
cricket lifts his wing-covers and draws the
scraper of one across the file of the other,
and thus sets both in vibration.   In order
to play on this natural violin the little
virtuoso is obliged to lift his upper wings in
a way that gives him a fierce and bristling

FIG. 10. Wing-
cover of Male
Cricket. File
enlarged.

appearance, quite at variance with his amorous tune
and frame of mind.   While the earlier songs of the

FIG. 11.　When the Afternoon Shadows in the Orchard lengthen.

cricket are for wooing, I have come to believe that the later songs of the autumn are made for the love of music.   Possibly he still plays on for the delectation of his mate, although the time of youth and love have passed by.   At all events, after the mating season is gone, you may hear these indefatigable serenaders from the hour when the afternoon shadows in the orchard lengthen until late at night, playing as steadily as if

they thought music the most important of occupations.

FIG. 12.   Ear of Cricket.

The cricket ear is placed most conveniently in the tibia of the front leg, so that these insects literally hear with their elbows. Figure 12 shows the ear of a cricket.   The katydids and meadow grasshoppers have their ears placed similarly.

The last but by no means least of our minnesingers is the snowy tree-cricket, the brave little musician of frosty autumn.   You will hear him first as you stroll along some country highway that leads past woods and orchard, and loses itself over dreamy hills set in the amethyst haze of September afternoons.[1]   His music is so much a part of the landscape that you have perhaps never noticed it at all, and certainly you have never seen this shy fiddler.   He lives mostly on trees and shrubs and is seldom visible because of his pallid green

[1] See Frontispiece.

color, which makes him seem a ghost of an insect rather than a real one. Figure 13 shows a male of the species; his fiddle is in structure similar to that of the black cricket. He is a true ventriloquist, and it is almost impossible to find him by following the seeming direction of his song.

There are two species of snowy tree-crickets common in eastern United States which resemble each other so closely in appearance that only an entomologist's trained eye can distinguish them. However, their music is totally different. I remember well a certain September when I was associated with two entomologists who spent most of their leisure in a patient

Fig. 13. Snowy Tree-cricket.

and loving study of the habits of these two species. One they named " the whistler " and the other " the fiddler." The whistler is oftener found on low shrubs or in the grass, and he gives a clear, soft, prolonged, unbroken note. The fiddler's note is louder and short and continuously repeated. To the listener it soon seems like a refined and gentle imitation of the katydid's song. There seem to be three notes, the first and third being accented, "Ka′-ty did′." But when studied more closely we are not sure whether the accent is in the music or in the listener's imagination; and, finally, in bewilderment we simply accept the fact that somehow there is a delightful rhythm in it and cease trying to analyze it. We also note that this singer's vivacity is dependent upon warm temperature.

So far as we know, this snowy tree-cricket is the only one of the insect musicians that seems conscious of the fact that he belongs to an orchestra. If you listen on a September evening, you will hear the first player begin; soon another will join, but not in harmony at first. For some time there may be a see-saw of accented and unaccented notes; but after a while the two will be in unison; perhaps not, however, until many more players have joined the concert. When the rhythmical beat is once established it is in as perfect time as if governed by the baton of a Damrosch or a Thomas. The "throbbing of the cricket heart of September" it has been fitly named. Sometimes an injudicious player joins the chorus at the wrong beat, but he soon discovers his error and rectifies it. Sometimes, also, late at night, one part of the orchestra in an orchard gets out of time with the majority, and discord may continue for some moments, as if the players were too cold and too sleepy to pay good attention. This

delectable concert begins usually in the late afternoon and continues without ceasing until just before
dawn the next morning.   Many times I have heard
the close of the concert ; with the " wee sma " hours
the rhythmic beat becomes slower ; toward dawn there
is a falling off in the number of players ; the beat is
still slower, and the notes are hoarse, as if the fiddlers
were tired and cold ; finally, when only two or three are
left, the music stops abruptly.   Fitly and fortunately
the song of this cricket is the most soothing of all the
songs of insects.   To listen to it consciously would
make the most unfortunate victim of insomnia drowsy.
It is the incarnation in sound of the spirit of slumber ;
it broods over the care-tired world, and with gentle
insistence hushes it to sleep.

Fig. 14.   A Restful, Woodsy Path.

II

A LITTLE NOMAD

NE warm August morning I followed a certain restful, woodsy path which soon led me to a partially wooded hillside. I found a shady resting-place under a pair of twin maple trees, where I settled contentedly in the grass with some downy young sumacs for neighbors. The blue waters of the lake twinkled up at me through the tree-boles, and a blue sky beamed down on me through the tree-tops. The breeze, playing softly with the leaves above me, and the soft swish of the water on the rocks below united in a soothing song, to which a cicada from his high perch was doing his best to perform a worthy obligato. I was tired of a world of work and care ; and as I turned my footsteps toward this cosy nook I said to myself, " I will go where I can be alone." Vain decision and absurd desire ! I had just arranged for myself a tree-trunk chair-back and was enjoying the nice bark upholstery when a grandfather graybeard came teetering along on his stilts, letting his body down at rhythmic intervals to feel of my hand with his palpi to discover if perchance I were good to eat. Then a red squirrel darted up a young ash tree in front of me, the dark stripe on his side where the red and white meet being particularly vivid and dashing; at first he sneezed and coughed his displeasure at my intrusion and then sprang his rattle so suddenly that I wondered if it might be that squirrels have secreted in them storage batteries that may be switched at will from action to sound. Then a great butterfly, a tiger swallowtail, came careening down through a hole in my leaf canopy and alighted on a sunlit bush near me; there, in utter luxuriousness, he slowly opened and shut his wings in obvious enjoyment of his sun-bath. While watching him I noticed that the maple sapling, on which he was resting, was in a bad way; its leaves were riddled with holes, varying in size from that of a bird shot to that of a small bean.

Now while I was tired of a world that lectured and talked and argued and did many other noisy things that wore on one's nerves, I was by no means tired of the great silent world that did things and made no fuss about doing them. So, when my butterfly drifted away, I lazily began to investigate the cause of the dilapidation of the maple leaves. There I found, as I suspected at first glance, a little nomad

Fɪɢ. 15.   Twin Maples.

named the Maple-leaf Cutter, which pitches its tent
on leafy plains and whose acquaintance I had made

Fig. 16.   Maple-leaf Cutter : Moth and Camping-ground of Caterpillar.

several years ago when I was employed to make its
family portraits.

I plucked a leaf that had several oval holes in it and

also several oval rings marked by a tracing of bare veins and translucent leaf tissue (Fig. 16); then I noticed an oval bit of leaf wrong side up on the upper surface of the leaf. A glance at this through my lens showed that it was made fast to its place by several bundles of glistening white silk. With a knife point I tore asunder these ropes and lifted the wee tent and found fastened to its under surface another bit of the leaf identical in shape but somewhat smaller. Suddenly from an opening between the two an inquiring head was thrust out with an air that said plainly, " Who's there? " I tore the two pieces of leaf apart to get a better view of the little inmate. He was a stocky, brownish caterpillar, about one-sixth of an inch long, with shields on his thoracic seg-ments that shone like polished bronze

Fig. 17. Caterpil-lar of Maple-leaf Cutter enlarged.

and an anal shield that was dull purple (Fig. 17). His several simple eyes were in two such compact groups that they gave the impression of two keen, beady, black eyes, and I had a feeling that he was inspecting me through the lens. He was very unhappy and squirmy when removed from his cover, and he backed so vigorously that he backed half his length out of the rear end of his tent before he

felt safe, and then remained very still. His loosened
tent was lying bottom side up on the leaf; and owing
to my clumsy proportions I was obliged to leave the
labor of righting it to him; he gave it his immediate
attention and went at it in a most workmanlike
manner. He crawled halfway out upon the leaf and
by a dexterous lift of the rear end of his body he
brought the tent down right side up and at once
began pegging it down. To do this he moved his

lower lip around and around on the
leaf surface to make fast, then spun
his rope up and lifting his head
fastened it to the edge of the tent;
this process he repeated many times,
but with great rapidity, and when
the fastening was finished it was
well worth seeing. He had spun his

Fig. 18. Tent Ropes of
the Maple-leaf Cutter.

silken cords so they formed an X.
This arrangement allowed him room
to fasten many lines to the leaf and tent, and since
they were crossed in the middle they had the strength
of many twisted strands (Fig. 18). He put his first
fastening at one side of his tent and then hastened to
put another on the opposite side, and thus made secure
he took his time for putting down the remainder of his
ropes.

While watching him spin, I mused on his history as revealed in its earlier chapters by that truly great scientist, Dr. Fitch, and added to in its later chapters by our own Dr. Lintner, — two men of whom New York is so justly proud. This history was as follows: Last May a tiny moth (*Paraclemensia acerifoliella*) sought out this maple sapling; she was a beautiful little creature with a wing expanse of a little more than a half inch; her front wings and thorax were steel-blue, and her hind wings and abdomen were pale, smoky brown; these hind wings were bordered with a wide, fine fringe; across both sets of wings glinted and gleamed a purple iridescence like that on the surface of a bit of mother-of-pearl. On her head, between her antennæ, she wore a little cap of orange feathers, this color combination of orange and steel-blue proving her to be a moth of fine discrimination in the matter of dress. This pretty mother moth laid an egg upon the leaf which I held in my hand; from that egg hatched my wee caterpillar, and began life, I suspect, as a true leaf-miner. However, this is a guess of my own, inspired by the appearance of the leaf. Anyway, he did not remain a miner long, but soon cut out a bit of the leaf and pulled it over him and pegged it down; beneath it he pastured on the green leaf-tissues in safety, and in this retreat he shed his skin. With added growth came

the need for more commodious quarters ; so he cut
another oval piece from the leaf, as much larger than
his tent as he could reach without coming entirely out
of his cover ; before he cut it completely free he ingen-
iously fastened one side of it to the leaf with silk so that
he would not fall, cradle and all, to the ground.   He
then used this fastening as a hinge as he came part way
out of his tent, took a good hold of the leaf with his
sharp claws, and flipped the loosened piece over his back

and fastened it down over fresh feed-
ing-ground.   What was previously his
tent was then a rug beneath him ; his
new pasture was a margin of about
one-twelfth inch that lay between the
edges of his rug and his tent ; for he
was ever averse to exposing his precious person to lurking enemies more
than was strictly necessary.   Before
he shed his skin again he may have
needed a new pasture ; if so, he struck

Fig 19.   A Lilliputian
Mud-turtle.

his tent and walked off with it on his back, looking like
a Lilliputian mud-turtle, and finally fastened it on a new
site (Fig. 19).   He had already several times gone through
this process of upsetting his house, for he had two rugs
beneath him and two tents above him of graduated sizes.
And I knew that some time in the near future he would

peg down his largest tent more securely than he had ever done before, and there in this safe shelter would change to a pupa. When the leaf that had been the range of this small nomad fell in the autumn he would go with it; and wrapped in his tent rugs he would sleep his winter sleep under the snow until he should awaken next spring, no longer a tenter on leafy plains, but a true child of the air.

I tore off a bit of the leaf on which my little friend had settled, and went over and pinned it to a leaf still on the bush. It may have been an absurd thing to do, but by this time I was shamelessly, nay, intrepidly sentimental, and I did not wish that little chap to starve because of my inborn tendency to meddle with other people's affairs. I then fell from bad to worse and began to moralize; for when a naturalist falls to moralizing science weeps. I meditated thus, " I came here to get away from puzzling problems, and yet here they are all around me; the problems of the little nomad; the problems of the poor, leaf-lacerated maple; and if I look in other directions I will find more in plenty." But for some sweet reason I did not feel about problems as I did when I ran away and hid from the noisy world two hours before. I was filled with a new sense of the dignity and grandeur of this great silent struggle for adjustment and supremacy which

was going on around me. I felt inspired to go back
and serenely do my own little part as well as I
could, trusting that somehow, somewhere, and to
Some One the net proceeds of struggle are greater than
the cost.

III

A SHEEP IN WOLF'S CLOTHING

TO hatch from the egg, to attain growth through steady attention to eating, to reach maturity and produce eggs for another generation, are the necessities of insect life. The ways and means of accomplishing these things successfully is a problem which is partially solved by the habits of the species, and partially by the efforts of the individual. The habits of a species comprise the wisdom stored up in the experience of that species during thousands of years; the habits of a species is the pathway by which it has struggled up to the ranks of the " fittest " which have survived.

No insect history better epitomizes the history of a race than does that of the Viceroy Butterfly (*Limenitis archippus*), a beautiful insect which in early summer makes our open fields and marshy meadows brilliant with the flashing of orange-red wings in the sunshine. The early stages of the Viceroy have been worked out in detail and given to the world through the careful and patient labors of Dr. S. H. Scudder.

Fig. 20.   The Home of the Young Viceroy.

The Viceroy mother selects usually the terminal twigs of some willow or poplar, and places her eggs singly on the tips of the terminal leaves (Fig. 20). Now this choice of the topmost leaf of the branch is not without reason on the part of the mother. This egg, though scarcely so large as a pinhead, has many enemies ; there are spiders always prowling around to find tidbits for their rapacious stomachs; there are tiny ichneumon-flies ready to lay their eggs within even so small an egg as this; there are wasps and other voracious insects always on the lookout for things eatable. So there is reason for putting these eggs one in a place on the tip end of a branch, where the wind always keeps the leaves stirring in a way to confuse the vision of these active foes. As a protection against these same inquisitive eyes the egg is of a dark green color, almost the exact hue of the upper surface of the leaf on which it is invariably placed. This little green egg is a beautiful object when viewed through a microscope ; it is ornately sculptured in an hexagonal pattern and set with short spines. It seems to be one of nature's laws of beauty that nothing is too small to be worth while.

After from four to eight days have elapsed since the egg was laid, a little brownish larva gnaws its way out through the side. As soon as it is fairly out it turns around and eats the egg-shell, carving, spines, and all.

Not for sentiment nor yet for digestion does the larva perform this somewhat auto-cannibalistic feat; but for the very practical reason that the empty shell if left

Fig. 21.   Viceroy Caterpillar on Bare Midrib behind Decoy Bundle at A ; B, Winter Home of Viceroy Caterpillar.

would mayhap yield a clew to his enemies which they might follow up to his undoing.   Then the little caterpillar begins feeding across the end of his native leaf, leaving the midrib untouched.   Maybe the midrib is too tough for the jaws of a baby caterpillar. On the other hand, his subsequent actions would seem to imply method in his manner of attacking the leaf ; for the Viceroy larva is a night feeder, and he uses the denuded midrib as a perch during the day. Stretched out lengthwise on this he is nearly invisible during his earlier stages. Besides this, he uses a very ingenious device to distract the attention of keen eyes from his precious person ; he fastens with a silken thread a little bunch of débris to the bare stem between his feeding-place and his resting-place (Fig. 21). This is a clever performance ; for if one of his foes should be hunting on this leaf and should start out on the denuded stem it would meet with this empty and worthless mass and would naturally be discouraged from further investigation. As the caterpillar gnaws off more of the leaf he moves his ambush bundle farther down the stem ; so it is evidently of some real use to him.

After a few days our caterpillar finds his skin too small for his increasing size and proceeds to shed it caterpillar-wise ; but he is still unwilling to leave any traces of himself around, so he eats up his old skin as he did his egg-shell. He soon destroys the leaf of his birth and then consumes others. In the course of his growth he sheds his skin three times and after each moult he assumes a change of form and color. Various

warts and tubercles appear on him after the first moult;
these grow more numerous and noticeable with each
succeeding change until he becomes a most grotesque
and amazing-appearing creature, with a pair of spiny
pompons in front and spines too numerous to mention
decorating his body.   Most people not entomologically
educated would exclaim on seeing this caterpillar when
full grown " The horrid thing ! "   And if the caterpillar
could hear and be conscious of the history of his race

as embodied in himself, he
would rejoice and be exceed-
ing glad over this verdict ; for
it is greatly to his advantage
now to look so disagreeable

Fig. 22.   " So humpy and spiny
that no bird would touch him."

that no one would willingly
molest him.   The height of his
racial ambition is to be so humpy and spiny that no bird,
however rash, would dare to touch him.   His coloring
now is pale olive, with a large white blotch in the middle
so as to make him resemble a bit of bird-lime on a leaf.
Not only in color and shape is he ugly, but he seeks to
intimidate by his movements any approaching enemy.
When he walks his head trembles as if he had the palsy,
making the whole leaf quake and likewise the heart of
the foe.   If he is attacked or disturbed, he will fly into
a tremendous rage and swing his head from one side to

the other in a ferocious fashion. Mr. Scudder saw two
of these caterpillars meet, and each began a great
swinging of the head, hitting the other several times
during this family jar. When fully grown the caterpillar, if disturbed, moves his head around in a circle on
the leaf and " gnashes his teeth " in fury. To one who
understands him this is a very funny bluff; for he is
not only absolutely harmless, but he is also very fastidious about his food and could not be in-
duced to take a bite out of an assailant.

When the Viceroy changes to a chrysalis he is almost as grotesque in form as
when he was a larva; for he now wears
a large excrescence in front that bears a
resemblance to a Roman nose (Fig. 23).
The obvious use of this protuberance is to

Fig. 23. " An un-
even morsel."

convince a bird of the utter futility of attempting to
swallow such an uneven morsel.

About a month after the egg is laid the adult insect
appears, and on gorgeous wings sails off to join its
fellows; for this is a social butterfly and is fond of
dancing about in the air with its comrades.

Very soon are the eggs laid for another brood. But
the history of an individual of this generation is very
different in some particulars than the one just related.
After a larva of the second brood hatches, he feeds, as

did his parent, on the tip of the leaf, leaving the midrib for a perch during the day. But when he is about
one-third grown he commences to display a peculiar
interest in a certain, chosen leaf. He first fastens
the petiole to the branch by weaving around the two
many strands of silk; this is to keep the leaf from
falling when assailed by the fierce winds of autumn.
He then proceeds to the tip of the leaf and gnaws it
off squarely across, leaving the midrib bare as usual;
he is a clever engineer and leaves just enough of the
leaf to suit his purpose. He folds the remaining portion of the leaf into a tube and sews it with a neat
silken seam and then lines the tube luxuriously with
silk (Fig. 21, *B*). The little house thus made is just
large enough for the insect's body; and he crawls
into it, his warty last segment fitting nicely the orifice
and constituting a living door. The question at once
suggests itself, how does this larva know how to do
this thing? His parents did not do it, and if he
inherited the knowledge it must have been from his
grandparents. This is one of the inscrutable mysteries;
and all we know about it is that during the warm days
of autumn, long before there is any hint of winter in
even the skies, this caterpillar, which never experienced
a winter and whose parents never experienced a winter,
builds himself this winter house and hides himself

within it. Moreover, he selects a leaf near the ground
so that he may have the protection of a cover of snow,
which proves him to be truly winter-wise. He and all
his generation pass the winter safely in their tiny tene-
ments, remaining there dormant until the first buds
or catkins of the spring call them to a vernal break-

Fig. 24. The Viceroy.

fast; then they back out of their dwellings and devote
themselves thereafter to eating and growing as if they
had never experienced a winter vacation while pursu-
ing this important business. They change to butterflies
in June.

The flight of the Viceroys consists of a few rapid
flutters of the wings and then a period of sailing
through the air with wings extended. This exposes
them mercilessly to the attack of birds which regard

most butterflies as the most delectable sort of food.
This butterfly is especially agreeable as a diet to birds,
and yet they rarely touch it. Why is this? It is
another instance of the marvellous adaptation of this
species to its environment, and of its power to seize
an advantage in a precarious situation. This wonder-

Fig. 25.   The Monarch.

ful little creature that resembled disagreeable things
when it was young to save itself from being eaten by
birds, now, when grown, resembles in color and markings a butterfly which birds avoid for good reason.
This butterfly (*Danaus plexippus*) is named the Monarch,
and it belongs to a group all members of which are
nauseous to birds. Its gay color, orange-red marked

with black borders and veins, is its protection; for it is an advertisement, a sort of a poster which proclaims that here is something that right-minded birds leave alone. So our palatable Viceroy has developed colors and markings so nearly like the unpalatable Monarch that no feathered creature will touch him, unless perchance one shall be knowing enough to notice the black band across the Viceroy's hind wings which is his chief distinguishing mark.

To understand the magnitude of the feat accomplished by the Viceroys in abjuring their family colors of black, white, and blue, and adopting the orange and black uniform of the Monarchs we must consider the vast differences in the earlier stages of the two species. The Monarch egg is laid upon the tender terminal leaves of milkweed and is quite as ornate as that of the Viceroy but of quite different pattern. When the caterpillar hatches, it pursues the same tactics as does that of the Viceroy; and for the same wise precaution eats its egg-shell. The milkweed is a succulent food, and the caterpillar may mature in eleven days; when full grown it is a gay creature banded crosswise with black, yellow, and green; on the second segment of the thorax and the seventh segment of the abdomen are a pair of black, flexible, whiplike filaments. They are smug-looking caterpillars, and they are smug in spirit also, for they are permeated with a race consciousness that the more they flaunt their gay stripes to the world the less likely are they to be attacked by a prudent bird. It is a great advantage to an insect to have the bird

FIG. 26. "Smug-looking caterpillars."

problem eliminated from the start. However, there remains the problem of parasites and, therefore, the black whips. When I was a child I disturbed a flock of these caterpillars resting together on the lower side of a leaf of milkweed, and I still remember the creepy fascination with which I gazed at the black and yellow ringed creatures and the waving, jerking whips lashing back and forth to frighten away ichneumons; if the real ichneumons were as frightened as I was, the caterpillars were surely safe.

The chrysalis of the Monarch is the most beautiful gem in nature's casket of living jewels. Its color is the most exquisite green, and it is enamelled with dots of shining gold; a gold far more wonderful than was ever mined by man. This ornamentation can be of no real use to the insect, and one is driven again to the conclusion that nature has so wrought this living jewel for the sake of beauty alone.

From this emerald case comes, in due time, the great red-winged butterfly; and how so large a butterfly can be packed in so small a case is nothing less than a miracle. If, perchance, the issuing butterfly is a male, then we have before us the veriest of insect dandies; he is not only trig in figure and gorgeous in color but on each hind wing he carries a sachet bag embroidered in black. He indulges in no vulgar flirting of a scented handkerchief to allure his lady-love; he simply flirts a beauteous red wing with a perfume pocket on it, and lo! she is won.

But the Monarchs have other problems of their own just because the bird problem is eliminated. For because of this immunity they spread and flourished in their native tropic America until there came the problem of more food plants, more milkweed. And thus they began pushing farther north and south during the seasons of milkweed growth. As they could not endure the northern winter they simply came north for the summer and went back for the winter. At least this is what the wise men tell us. But this northern migration is carried on in a most peculiar manner. Each mother butterfly follows the spring northward as it advances as far as she finds the milkweed sprouted. There she deposits her eggs, from which hatch individuals that carry on the journey and lay their eggs as far to the north as possible ; perchance it is their children that we hear of in late summer on the shores of Hudson Bay. As cool weather approaches the Monarchs gather in vast flocks for the southward migration. These flocks are not made up of the individuals that migrated north but of their children and grandchildren. There are no old ones among them travel-wise to guide them back to Florida and the West Indies. How they know the way is beyond our imagination, unless, perhaps, there flows in their bodies tropical blood that impels them to go back where the bamboo shades the stream, and the torn banners of the banana wave on sluggish breeze. All we know is this : the Monarchs migrate northward by generations and southward by individuals ; and from Patagonia to Athabasca swings the migratory pendulum. Nor is it content with this range ; the strongest flier of all the butterflies it hesitates not to try its for-

tune over seas, and has been found flying bravely
five hundred miles from shore.   Either by flight or
as stowaways in vessels they have pressed eastward
to western Europe and westward to the farthest
isles of the Pacific.   Well is it named the "Monarch,"
for it is the most daring and indomitable butterfly that
we know, pushing back its geographical boundaries to
the very edge of the Arctic zone, and exploring on
leisurely and confident wing the seas that wash the
shores of the Occident and Orient.

No wonder the Viceroy chose so splendid a creature
to imitate.   But I fear there is little noble ambition
as a motive to the imitation; just to keep alive as a
species is all.   The value of such mimicry seems
a part and parcel of the Viceroy's equipment with
which to march in the ranks of the fittest.   In
southern Florida a common butterfly is a species of
the bad-tasting family to which the Monarch belongs;
this is a dark mahogany-brown butterfly with no black
veins and borders.   Therefore, in Florida, our imitative
Viceroy doffs his stolen uniform of orange and black
and dons another stolen uniform of mahogany-brown.
He evidently chooses his liveries for safety and not for
their intrinsic beauty; and he is entirely satisfied as
long as he successfully masquerades in a guise that
shall deceive the keen eyes of the birds of the air.

Fig. 27.   Olden Cities.

IV

THE PERFECT SOCIALISM

IT is unquestionable that the word "socialist" is an epithet of reproach in the popular mind, and is associated with attempts
to subvert the law and order of civilized
society. Yet the student of history is
bound to confess that socialism has been
the product of the highest civilization. In every form it
has been an attempt, however misguided, to insure the
good of society at large through curtailing and regulating
the rights of the individual. The underlying idea of
socialism has ever been to secure for man upon earth the
equal chances for happiness which, it is believed, God in
his justice grants to man in the next world. The popular
disrepute of socialism is doubtless due, in part, to various unsuccessful experiments in communal life; but it
is due also to the individualism of the human race,
which rebels against any levelling tendency. We each
prefer to keep our own fighting chance, however poor,
to sharing the same with our fellows less fortunate in
endowment and environment.

It is strange that in the history of socialism the fact has been disregarded that, thousands of years before Saint-Simon, Fourier, Owen, and Karl Marx lived and wrote, insects had already solved the problems of practical socialism. Surely, had Solomon been as interested in social experiments as he was in industrial progress he would have said, " Go to the ant, thou socialist, learn her ways of community life and be wise ; for she provideth her meat in the summer, and gathereth her food in the harvest, and shareth freely with her fellows the products of her labors."

The successful socialists among insects are bees, ants, and wasps, all of which belong to the order Hymenoptera. But, as if to show that the lines of social development in the insect world are founded upon fundamental law, we find another group of insect socialists, the white ants, or termites, which belong to an entirely different order. They differ as much structurally from the ants, bees, and wasps as do men from horses, and yet their social habits are much the same. And even within the Hymenoptera the social habits of bees, wasps, and ants have doubtless been developed independently.

Let us examine the claims insects have to be ranked as socialists and see if they are not well founded. The efforts of human socialists have been directed toward non-competitive division of labor, united capital, communal habitations, and amalgamation of interests. All these conditions and more are to be found in insect societies; for the social insects are uncompromising Malthusians and rigorously control the increase ot population. We will discuss these claims in detail and see how they are substantiated by the facts observed in the insect world.

Caste

Division of labor by caste is a most interesting phase of insect socialism and deserves to be considered first. Our little six-footed brethren have loosed the Gordian knot of division of labor through creating castes more immutable than those of the Brahmins, and they have solved the problems of caste by making their existence a benefit to the whole society instead of to the individuals belonging to the caste. This is brought about by making each caste represent a division of labor based upon the needs of the whole community. The castes are: queens, kings, workers, and soldiers, and a study of the functions of each is necessary in order to understand the economy of the insect commune.

Royalty

The term " queen " is a misnomer among insects, for they have no rulers in their societies. The queen is always the mother of the colony, and the devoted attention she receives is due to the fact that without her the community would perish.

The queen has reached her highest development in the honey-bee, and we will study her there. From infancy she is destined to maternity, and her life-history is briefly as follows : When the workers wish to develop a queen they tear down the partitions between three adjacent cells containing eggs which would naturally develop into workers. They destroy two of the eggs, reserving the third as occupant of the large cell which they proceed to build over it. The egg hatches into a little white bee grub, in no wise differing from those in the neighboring cells. But soon the process of differentiation begins, for this grub is fed upon a highly nutritious food, made by the workers, called "royal jelly." Not for the delectation of the babe in the royal cell is she fed royal jelly, but because this rich diet has a marvellous effect upon her physical development, giving her great capabilities for producing eggs. For five days she is fed upon this stimulating food, and then the workers cap her cell and leave her alone to change to a pupa.

About sixteen days from the date of hatching, the queen is ready to come out of her cell ; the workers know this and are ready to open the cell and help the royal lady out, now in full possession of her legs and wings. In appearance she is larger than the largest workers — evidently a queenlier bee. Her first act, if unhindered by the workers, is her one claim to similarity to human royalty : she starts at once on a hunt for other queens in the hive, for our queen is jealous and will brook the presence of no other claimant to her throne. Her sting is a noble weapon kept sacred to the slaying of her peers. She hunts for other queen-cells, tears them open with great fury, and assassinates the helpless young princesses within them. But she is quite as ready for fair fight as for assassination, for when she finds another queen fully developed she will fight her until one or the other is killed. The stark bodies of fifteen unfortunate queens we found one day thrown out of one of the hives; grim witnesses to the prowess of the royal lady in possession of the colony.

In a few days after maturity the queen takes her marriage flight in the sunshine. As soon as she returns from her honeymoon the queen proceeds at once to business, moving around upon the comb and gluing her eggs to the bottoms of the cells. When the honey season is at its height she works with great rapidity, sometimes laying eggs at the rate of six per minute, accomplishing the feat of laying over three thousand eggs per day — nearly twice her own weight. She is a wise queen, moreover, and has an eye to the dangers of overpopulation. When there is much honey and great activity on the part of the workers and the swarming season is at hand she enlarges her empire rapidly; but when there is little honey she takes care that the population be limited to practical numbers. Whether she does this as the result of her wisdom, or whether she is guided by the quality of food the workers give her, is a mooted question. From the point of this discussion it matters not whether it be queen or subjects that evince such foresight; the fact that interests us is that the bee socialists do control population.

The queen also coöperates with the workers in determining the relative proportions of the two sexes. The workers are developed in comb composed of small cells, the drones in comb composed of larger cells. The greater part of the comb in the brood chamber is of the first type, as it is essential that the greater number of bees reared be workers. But as the swarming season approaches the workers provide comb made up of the larger cells, unless there is already a sufficient quantity in the hive. This constitutes the workers' part in determining the relative proportion of the sexes in the colony; it remains for the queen to complete the work. In the smaller cells she deposits eggs that will develop into workers, and in the larger cells only those that will develop into drones.

The queen bee could never accomplish such feats in egg-laying if she were not cared for with great solicitude by the workers. Her powers of motherhood are developed at the expense of the rest of her physique. Her stomach is not fitted for the process of digestion; she is always fed upon digested food, and thus her energies are conserved for her great task.

Often in the summer or fall swarms of winged ants may be encountered by the unhappy traveller, who has much to do to keep them out of his eyes and mouth. These winged forms are the king and queen ants taking their marriage flight. As soon as this wedding tour is over they drop to the ground; the kings die soon, the queens tear off their wings in a great hurry, and, like the queen bee, go to work at once. The first eggs the queen ant lays she takes care of herself, housing and feeding the young in a true, motherly way. The first brood is composed of workers, and after their maturity they take care of the nest and the young, and the energies of the queen are reserved for the production of eggs. In one particular is the queen ant more amiable than the queen bee: she suffers no throes of jealousy and dwells in peace with other queens in the nest. The worker ants evidently regulate the size of the royal family.

The kings and queens of the termites take flight at

first as do the ants. The queen and king are adopted into some colony, where they are carefully cared for, a royal cell being fashioned for their use. The queen becomes greatly developed in size, until her abdomen is a great egg sac, sometimes six or seven inches long. Of course she cannot move, but lives in imprisoned helplessness, finding her only relief in the devotion of her consort and subjects.

It is a sorry part in the larger affairs of the insect world that is played by the males, whether we call them kings or drones. Much scorn has been heaped upon drones because they are the idlers in the bee commune, but surely their lot is the least enviable of all the castes in the hive. The drone's sole *raison d'être* is to be consort of the queen; but as there are hundreds of drones to one queen, naturally there are very few that fill the office intended for them by nature. Even if one is successful, he loses his life for love; while the many unsuccessful kings without kingdoms are mercilessly sentenced to death by their worker sisters as soon as the honey supply runs low. Cheshire describes the killing of drones thus : —

" No sooner does income fall below expenditure than their nursing sisters turn their executioners, usually by dragging them from the hive, biting at the insertion of the wing. The drones, strong for their special work,

FIG. 28. An Ant Town.

are after all as tender as they are defenceless, and but little exposure and abstinence is required to terminate their being. So thorough is the war of extermination that no age is spared! ''

The question as to the economy of developing so many useless princes royal is a puzzling one, and can only be explained by the theory that natural selection has acted to preserve those colonies having many drones — another instance of the flagrant waste of individuals for the benefit of the race. I call to mind a slaughter of drones I once witnessed in an observation hive. The openings in the hive were large enough to admit the workers only and therefore too small to allow the passage of the bodies of the drones; so the determined workers spent several days in tearing their wretched victims limb from limb and removing them in sections. Below a small crevice at the bottom of the hive could be seen a windrow of disjointed legs and wings torn from the poor drones. The king ants die natural deaths, if death from cold and starvation may be called so ; at least, they are not subject to assassination as are the king bees. The king termite is a noted exception in the insect world, as he lives a long and exemplary life, sharing with his queen the attention and devotion of his subjects.

Devotion to royalty has been much misunderstood by

the earlier writers. Lubbock and McCook, as well as apiarists, have shown that the devotion to the queen is a matter of business interests to the colony. Not her royal body do they revere but her royal prerogative of motherhood. " What does " is the criterion of socialists; " what is " counts for nothing. Ants show a great deal of devotion to a dead queen, giving her attention for days or even weeks after her death. While the queen bee moves about freely in the hive, the queen ant has a bodyguard which always accompanies her and often restricts her movements.

Beekeepers often have occasion to introduce new queens into hives that are queenless. This is a delicate undertaking, and many expedients are resorted to in order to accomplish it successfully. It is interesting to note the manner in which the bees refuse to accept a strange queen. They " ball " her, as it is called; i.e. a great number of workers cluster close around her, making a compact ball about the size of an egg, and thus delicately smother her royal highness with much attention. Getting rid of unwelcome royalty by the process of smothering is not unknown in our own annals. This method is probably adopted by bees through their instinct of never inflicting wounds upon an active queen; it is to be noted that if a queen bee is disabled, she is killed by ordinary methods and pitched out of the hive, thus showing conclusively that it is the function of royalty rather than the person that is respected.

THE WORKERS AND CITIZENS

The workers constitute by far the greater part of the insect societies; as their name implies, they carry on the industries and business affairs of the community. In the case of ants, bees, and wasps the workers are females whose reproductive organs are undeveloped. Among the termites the workers are both male and female, but with similarly rudimentary reproductive systems. Thus it seems that the bearing of young is found incompatible with business life in insect societies.

Not so, however, is the care of the young; this is always considered one of the most important of the industries of the commune. Among the bees and ants the care of the young is relegated to the younger sisters, although the elders do not scorn these duties if they find their performance necessary. The first work of the ant or bee just emerged from the pupa state is that of nurse, and a most tender and devoted one she is. Especially are the ant nurses solicitous about the health and comfort of their small charges. In some species the young ant grubs are assorted into sizes, those of the same age being kept in the same apartment, suggesting a graded school. When the ant babies are hungry they stretch up like young birds, and their nurses regurgitate partly digested food into the gaping, hungry mouths. The nurses keep them very clean by licking them with their long tongues, and, what is more interesting, are very careful to keep them in the right temperature. When the sun shines hot on the nest in the morning the nurses carry their charges to the lower compartments, but toward night they carry them again to the upper nurseries. The nurses show great interest in the young when they emerge from the pupa state, helping them to straighten out their newly freed antennæ and legs, then taking a hand at their education by leading them around the city and showing them the ways of the formic world.

All the members of the insect commune are shining lights in their devotion to the young. The moment an ant nest is attacked those citizens who are not detailed to fight the intruders will snatch up the babies and flee with them to places of safety; or when hard pressed will fight to the death for their protection. This is worthy of note, since it is not the mother instinct for saving her young but is a race instinct instead. It may be here stated that the objects popularly known as ants' eggs are not the eggs, but the young grub ants or pupæ; the eggs are too small to be seen well with the naked eye.

The more successful the insect colony, the greater the number of young. Consider once the labor of the bee nurses, who may have, in strong colonies, twelve thousand hungry babies to feed every day. The work of the young bees is truly onerous ; for they not only have to be children's nurses but also have to feed the queen and drones, construct the comb, cap the larvæ cells, keep the hive clean, and keep it well ventilated by a process of draughts set up by using their wings as fans.

To secure the food for the whole society occupies the time of the older and majority of the members of the colony. Among the bees the workers are physically modified for their labors. The hind legs are broadened and concave above, so as to form baskets for the carrying of pollen. Between the segments and the lower side of the abdomen are glands for the secretion of wax. Two segments of the hind legs are formed, so as to make forceps to remove the plates of wax after they are secreted.

One of the most taxing of the bee industries is the making of wax. Bees gorge themselves with honey, then hang themselves up in festoons, or curtains, to the hive, and remain quiescent for hours ; after a time wax scales appear, forced out from the wax pockets. The bees remove these scales with their natural forceps, carry the wax to the mouth, and chew it for a time, thus changing it chemically. Thus it may be seen that wax-making is a great expense to the colony, for it costs not only the time of the workers but it is estimated that twenty-one pounds of honey is required to make one pound of wax. As a matter of fact much of bee labor is that of the manufacturing chemist. Raw material does not suit their fastidious taste; thus all the honey, their chief food, they take from the nectaries of flowers as cane sugar, and in the honey stomach mix it with a secretion which changes it into grape sugar.

Bees are unwearying workers; they share with the workers of other insect societies an utter recklessness as to their own individual safety and preservation. When a bee goes out for honey she also collects pollen, so that she comes back heavily laden and flying low and slowly. It is no wonder that an ancient Greek writer, noting the pollen upon the legs of a laden bee, states that on Hymettus the bees tie little pebbles to their legs to hold them down. The lavish wastefulness of individual life is shown by the relative longevity of bees during the working and resting season. Those individuals matured in the fall will live eight or nine months, while in the height of the honey season a bee will wear herself out in a month.

The hours of labor among the ant workers are greater than among bees, as they have been observed working until late at night. Some of the species in hot countries wisely do their labor at night, resting in their nests during the heat of the day. There seems to be more originality and variety to the labors of ant workers than we find among bee workers. The foragers bring back a great variety of food for the house-keepers and the young. Certain species in dry coun-tries provision their nests for the winter. The ants perform Herculean labors while excavating their tunnels as well as when carrying great burdens of food. The worker ants have a delightful habit of taking naps when they are tired. McCook describes their sleeping positions thus : —

" Some are squatted down on their abdomens and last two pairs of legs ; some lie upon their sides ; some are resting upon the hind legs, standing on tip-toe ; some are crouched upon the earth with faces downward ; several are piled one on top of another." When they awaken they stretch and yawn in the most naïve and human manner. In an ant's nest one thing is most noticeable ; however crowded the galleries may be, and however much the ants may be obliged to crawl over and push each other, they do it with the utmost good nature. Another noticeable thing is the free way in which the foragers feed the hungry. An individual seldom asks in vain for food. In spite of the thriftiness, the instinct of sharing is stronger than the instinct of accumulation. The generosity of these insect citizens toward each other is an ideal which still lies beyond the horizon of accomplishment in the human world.

The termite workers are of both sexes, and their industry is such that they prove a terrible plague in the tropical countries, where they abound. Our native species tunnel their nests in wood, and are, in fact, very skilful engineers, for they build covered ways, under which they work. A feat not only of engineering skill but skill in reasoning came to our eyes in our own insectary. A piece of rotten wood tunnelled by termites was put on a formicary which consisted of a board surrounded by a moat filled with water. As the queens of our native termites have never been discovered, we are unable to keep these little creatures contented in artificial nests. Thus the ones under observation were always seeking avenues of escape. They tried the moat at every point. Finally they observed that one end of their nest-log projected out beyond the outer edge of the moat, although several inches above it. At once they commenced building a covered way straight down from the projecting end, thus bridging the hated ditch with neatness and despatch.

Division of labor is carried to extremes among the honey-ants. In this species there is a caste whose business it is to form reservoirs for the storing of food. The storage individuals receive all the honey which the workers bring in. The crop becomes much enlarged, until it distends the entire abdomen. One of these little honey vats looks like a large currant, with head, thorax, and legs attached to one side. These very accommodating citizens hang to the roofs of the galleries of the nests, and during seasons of famine give up to their hungry sisters their surplus honey.

The detailing of certain duties to certain individuals has been alluded to in the discussion of the use of young citizens as nurses. Among the leaf-cutter ants of Texas the citizens work in gangs or relays. Certain individuals climb the trees and cut off the leaves, which drop to the ground ; there they are gathered up by other individuals, who carry them to the nest. Mr. McCook reports seeing three divisions thus at work in one ant's nest. He has evidence also that in some species the ants work in divisions while excavating their underground tunnels. This shows that they have a comprehension of the value of economy in labor.

The driver ants of Africa form living bridges and ladders through individuals clinging to each other until the rope is long enough to reach the desired point.

The marching hordes behind pass over these living bridges.

In the nests of bees, ants, and wasps, sentinels are stationed at the entrances, who give alarm in case of attack. In one species of ants, who make the entrances to the nests very small, the sentinels use their own heads for the gates. The advantages of this living portcullis are obvious, as no enemy could surprise the nest without awakening the sentinel. Ants, as a general thing, are careful about closing their doors at night. Mr. McCook gives most interesting accounts of the duties of the gate-closers in the nests of the Occident ant. The gate-closers work both from the outside and inside; the last ones outside leaving a small opening through which they push into the nests, finishing the task from within. One of the species of slave ants defends its nest by throwing up earthworks at the gates, so as to impede the progress of the invaders.

Communal Wealth

The property of insect societies consists of their dwellings, stored food, live stock, and slaves. We are met at the outset with the question whether insects have a true sense of property. If property be defined as a legal right to the ownership, use, enjoyment, and disposal of a thing, then we have certainly much to prove. The laws of insect communes may only be known through the actions of the communists. To us it seems that their sense of property is such as characterizes primitive peoples, whose unwritten laws are defined by brute force. The haste with which the ants remove their youngsters in case of attack can scarcely be classed under the sense of property rights, although in no instance does the mother of the young act as their defender. The state cares for the children, and the state defends them. However, the situation is somewhat different when it comes to the question of stored food. The bees and the agricultural ants store up food in the summer for use in the winter. Our common ants use plant lice for their milch cows, and in all of these cases the owners show by their actions a clear sense of property rights.

That bees have this sense is shown through their actions in defending their stores from other plundering swarms. Bee-robbing usually takes place when there is little nectar to be taken from flowers, and probably hunger incites to ill-gotten gain. It is interesting to note that strong colonies are seldom attacked, the weaker ones being the victims. The fury with which the owners of the honey fight for its retention is sufficient, when once seen, to convince any doubter that bees, at least, have a sense of property. When the robbed swarm is overcome and the queen killed the bees will desert and join the robbers, and help carry their own stores to the hive of the marauders. This shows that it is a matter of property and not individual animosity which inspires them, otherwise they would fight to the death. Bee hunters say that when taking up a bee-tree, or a beehive for that matter, the bees will fight furiously until their comb is actually broken; then they give up, and, defeated and despairing, cluster on the broken comb, making no further effort to save themselves. There is something touching in the story of these brave little defenders of stores and home, and their utter discouragement when they see their treasure broken and ruined. " Taking up " bee-trees and beehives is a barbarous performance, and does not redound to the honor of man; and the thought of it quite reconciles one to all of the bee-stings inflicted upon human beings since time began.

Another sign of the sense of ownership of stored provision is the care given it by the harvester ants of Texas and India. These wise harvesters store their seeds in underground granaries for winter use. After the rains come, the grain, if let alone, would naturally germinate or become mouldy. The ants comprehend this, and when good weather comes again they bring the grain up and dry it in the hot sun, and then return it to the granaries.

The most interesting instance of food provision by the ants is given by Professor Wheeler, who has shown that the leaf-cutter ants of Texas cut and drag leaves into their nests for the sake of the edible fungus that grows upon them there; these ants are true mushroom growers.

Of all the property belonging to ants, probably the plant-lice are cared for with most forethought and intelligence. The fact that the ants used the aphids for milch cows was discovered nearly a century ago, but the special care they give to their live stock has been a subject of more recent study. Almost any one may have observed ants running up and down the trunks of trees and shrubs. It is no joy of climbing nor desire for a wide outlook that leads the ants to ascend trees, but because the leaves of the trees afford pasturage for their small cattle, the aphids. These little creatures exude voluntarily drops of a sweet liquid known as honey dew. The process of milking is this: the ant comes up to the aphid and pats it on the back with her antennæ, at which the flattered and pleased aphid gives forth the honey dew from the alimentary canal, which the ant eats with every sign of enjoyment. It might seem at first glance that the benefits of this relationship accrue only to the ants. However, this is not the case. The ants are fierce defenders of their flocks, and make it very uncomfortable for the many insect enemies of the aphids. Some species of ants build sheds over the aphids upon the trees (Fig. 29), and other species remove them to the safety of their own nests; but the special claim of

FIG. 29. An Ant Cow-shed.

the ants as aphid protectors lies in the care of the aphid eggs, which are shown as much attention as their own.

This habit of ants has proven of economic importance to our farmers of the middle west. One of the serious pests in that region is the corn-root plant-louse. Professor Forbes has demonstrated that these corn-root lice are absolutely dependent on the ants which live in the earth of the corn-fields. Ants fetch the last brood of aphids in the fall into their nests, and there the oviparous generation is developed, and the eggs are laid. The ants give these eggs great care, taking them into the deeper galleries during cold weather and fetching them to the surface in warm days. When the young aphids hatch, the ants take them and place them upon the roots of the young corn, and thus gain a nucleus for their summer herds. This shows a process of reasoning on the part of the ants, since they do not feed upon corn roots themselves, and yet seem to know that the aphids require this food.

MILITARY FORCES, SLAVERY, AND WAR

Only among termites is there a strictly soldier caste. To this belong both males and females, which are distinguished by having very large heads, armed with strong jaws. The soldiers never do any work for the colony, but hold themselves within the nest, ready to defend it in case of attack. Strike a termite nest with a stick and instantly the little workers, busy with construction, will disappear, and the soldiers will rush out pell-mell, ready to throw themselves upon the intruder. If they see no enemy, they retire, and their places are taken by the workers, who proceed to repair the nest with great rapidity. The soldiers have a habit of striking their great jaws against the wood of the nest, making a clicking sound ; the workers respond to this signal with a hiss. Some naturalists have believed this knocking by the soldiers was an assurance that the coast was clear. Some have believed that it was a command to hasten, as the workers seem to hustle about faster after hearing it. As the termites do not carry on wars, the termite soldier is a guard to the nest rather than an aggressive foe.

Among bees and ants the soldiers are workers imbued with the spirit of warriors; as they are all females they may well be called Amazons. Here the industrial energies of the peaceful citizen are changed into those of a fighting militia under provocations most human. In the history of all the battles of earth we have no records of more reckless bravery or more undaunted facing of death than we find in the battles of bees and ants. The recklessness of the individual for her own life is shown by the fact that a bee, ant, or wasp, will attack a man or a horse, single-handed, without a moment's hesitation.

So perfect is socialism among ants that even slavery is robbed of some of its evils. The question may well be asked why slavery should be needed when once a perfect socialism is established. This is answered by the fact that selfishness is in this case characteristic of the community rather than the individual. Slaves are of great economic importance to an ant colony, although the direct benefit to any individual in the ant-hill is not obvious.

When a slave-making colony sets out on an expedition for capturing slaves, the warriors march in solid column to the nests of the victims and throw them-

selves upon it with great fury. Their object, however, is robbery and not murder. They never attempt
to enslave the mature ants but take the young grubs
to be brought up in future slavery. They have no
intention of exterminating the slave colonies, and thus
shut off future supplies; therefore they do not kill
any more of the defenders than is necessary in order
to capture the larvæ. These young ones carried to
the nests of their captors are there cared for as ten-
derly as their masters' own, and when they reach the
adult age they work as cheerfully as they would have
done in their own nests. They share the *esprit de
corps* of their adopted country, as is shown by the
fact that when their masters return from a marauding
expedition laden with live booty the slaves rush out
to meet them joyfully and help them bring in the
stolen larvæ; but when the masters come home empty-
handed, the slaves are surly and sometimes even
refuse for a time to let them come back into the
nests.

That the object of slave-makers in carrying off the
young of the slave species is to get workers for their
own colony is clearly evinced by the modifications of
the habits of the masters made by the presence of
slaves in their nests. All the slave-making species
become more or less dependent upon their slaves.

Fig. 30.   The Dwelling of a Wasp Commune.

The tendency is for the slaves to do the work of the commune, leaving the fighting for their masters. The Amazon ants described by Huber have become so dependent on their slaves that they no longer have the ability to make their nests, feed their young, or even feed themselves. Huber made a famous experiment by putting thirty of the Amazons with their young in a box with some food. All of them were on the verge of starvation, and some were even dead, when Huber introduced one of the slaves, who immediately resuscitated the fainting Amazons by feeding them, took care of the young, and made a nest, and, single-handed, established order.

The Amazons had retained only the power of fighting, for they were still most skilful and intrepid warriors. An instance of their martial acumen is shown in this observation by Huber : When they attacked the nests of their usual slaves, the pacific negro ants, they made the onslaught in solid column, made sure of their booty, and then scattered in disorder, each reaching the home nest as best she could. The negro ants are not good fighters, so this method of retreat was feasible. When there were no negro nests to pillage, the Amazons enslaved the miner ants, who are brave and tenacious fighters and follow the foe to their own gates rather than give up their young to slavery. When the Amazons attacked the miner nests they not only approached in solid column, but retreated in solid column, being thus enabled to meet their assailants to better advantage and showing themselves possessed of strategic powers of no mean sort.

The reasons for war among social insects, so far as we may observe, are based upon a sense of ownership of property; *i.e.* robbery of stored food, taking of slaves, and infringement of territorial rights. The wars may exist between different colonies of the same species or between different species. Among ants the different species vary greatly as to bravery and skill in warfare. The battles are fought by hand-to-hand conflict, and as the pre-gunpowder battles in our own history were most deadly, so are these ant battles, which only stop when there are no more soldiers left to fight. The weapons of the ant warrior are always strong jaws and in some species a venomous sting; our common species have the power of forcibly ejecting on their foes the very irritating formic acid, a sort of emmet vitriol.

The most skilled fighters among the species of ants march to battle in a solid column; when once there the mêlée resolves itself into a series of duels. Two enemies, approaching each other, rear on their hind legs, throw acid on each other, and then close in deadly combat, each trying to cut the other in twain. Often when two are struggling thus help will arrive from either side ; then there is a trial of strength among many, and an effort to take prisoners. Woe to the captured warrior, for " no quarter to prisoners " is one of the laws of emmet wars, and death comes swiftly and surely to the stranger within the gates of an ant republic. As night falls upon the battle-field there is a retreat of the soldiers to their respective cities, but morning finds them at their posts again with valor undiminished. The carnage of these battles is terrible to behold. The field is strewn with the remains of the dead and dying ; two enemies are often found clenched in deadly embrace. The ant is the bulldog of the insect world : when she once gets hold she never lets go ; though she may be torn in twain, her jaws will not relax. Many an ant victor wears involuntarily all her life, as a trophy of her prowess, the head of her vanquished enemy firmly fixed by its jaws to her leg.

Communal Habitations

The architecture of social insects is remarkable in its skilful adaptation to the needs of the commune. For ages the beauty and regularity of honeycomb have been the wonder and delight of mathematicians, who have shown its economy by much computation. Some have claimed that the hexagonal cell was a matter of necessity, the result of pressure ; but as the bees start the cells at their bases in hexagonal shape, and as they hollow out in a triangular pyramid a perfect rhomb in the bottom of the cell, I think we must concede to them some powers of the geometrician. Surely no mansions made of marble carven by the hand of man are more wonderful or beautiful in their structure than a perfect honeycomb. The power of bees to take industrial advantage of a situation is shown by the readiness with which they use the commercial foundation-comb introduced by apiarists to save their bees the expense of wax-making.

Wasps were the first and original paper makers, and as geometricians and architects vie with their relatives, the bees. One has only to study the stories in that gray apartment house called a wasps' nest to be filled with admiration for the skill of the builders. The wasps build their nests of a material made by gathering bits of weather-worn wood and chewing them up, making a true paper pulp. These builders are equal to emergencies. Once we involuntarily unroofed a wasps' nest that was under a board. Several days later we discovered that the nest was well roofed by neat paper shingles. Never before, probably, had these wasps or their ancestors been called upon to roof a domicile, but these did this original work with evident knowledge of the principles of roof-construction.

Ants' nests vary greatly in form and method of building. The most familiar of these are our so-called ant-hills. Such a nest consists of deep underground galleries and is very well fitted for housing the commonwealth.

Of all the species of ants of the United States, the agricultural ants show the greatest skill in city building and municipal improvements. The most interesting of these are the so-called flat-disk nests. These disks mark the position of the underground nest, and vary in size from four to ten feet in diameter. They are level and hard, and kept free from all vegetation, except at certain seasons when a species of grass, upon whose seeds the ants feed, is allowed to grow. Near the centre of a disk are one or two openings; these gates open into vestibules below, from which galleries lead to a system of rooms arranged in regular stories. These rooms are used as granaries and nurseries, and the nest may extend several feet below the surface of the ground. From the disks radiate roads leading out into the fields. These roads are hard and smooth; they are two or three inches wide at the opening on the disk, and are sometimes sixty feet long; they are evidently made to facilitate the work of the harvesters when bringing home their grain. If, during the winter, when the ants

Fig. 31. Neighborly Communes.

are underground, there is a growth of any sort upon the disks, or roads, it is cut down in the spring and everything cleared up.

These ants, as observed by Mr. McCook, were skillful engineers when cutting down the tough grass. The twisting process was often resorted to in severing a stem; and the use of the lever seemed to be understood, as they were observed to cut a blade at its base, then climb it to the end, thus bending it over and completing the fracture. The food of these ants is grain of different kinds, which is gathered when ripe, taken to the granaries, hulled, and stored for winter use. These are the ants which take their seeds out to dry after the rains. The grass which they allow to grow on their disks is called " ant rice." The older observers believed that they planted it there, but this is not proven. However, they evidently find it useful, or they would destroy it as they do other grasses.

The Identity of Interests

The identity of interests in insect societies is shown in many ways; but perhaps in no better way than by the cheerfulness with which they feed each other and the good nature which they evince toward each other in their crowded nests when carrying on their common industries. Methods of communication approaching to language exist among social insects, but what they say or exactly how they say is as yet largely a mystery to us. They can inform each other of the discovery of food, as is shown by many experiments. Sentinels are enabled by some means to arouse and alarm a whole colony with great celerity. But perhaps nothing is so wonderful about them as their ability to recognize members of their own commonwealth. This is a power beyond our ken, and cannot be compared with our recognition of individuals. Lubbock has shown that ants of the same nest recognize each other after being separated for nearly two years; also that when pupæ are taken from a nest and matured in a strange colony they were still recognized when they were returned to their own people. He also divided an ants' nest before the eggs were laid, and let each half develop its own young. Then he brought the two halves together again, and young and old alike recognized each other as kindred. Lubbock also showed that ants were able to distinguish their own intoxicated friends from strangers likewise intoxicated. In this experiment the ants seemed greatly disturbed by the disgraceful condition of their fellows, but they carried them into the nest for further care, while they summarily dumped the drunken strangers into the moat.

MUNICIPAL SANITATION

Ants, bees, and wasps are exceedingly cleanly in their municipal arrangements. This cleanliness is necessary surely in such teeming cities. All dirt is removed from the nest and the dead are carefully disposed of. The bees throw their deceased outside the hive; but the ants show a leaning toward cemeteries some distance from the nests. The sight of the dead above ground seems to disturb an ant's sense of the fitness of things. Mrs. Treat has observed that the red, slave-making species never deposit the slaves with their own dead but have separate cemeteries for them.

Personal habits of social insects are also very cleanly; they brush and lick themselves with great assiduity. The bees have a special antennæ comb developed on the front leg, a circular aperture set with spines, through which the antennæ may be drawn. The ants have developed a regular comb in the form of a spur on the tibia of the front leg. This spur is set with strong spines, and is used by the ant exactly as we would use a comb and brush. Ants often lend a helping mandible or tongue to their fellows when performing toilet duties, amicably licking each other clean.

Ants carry each other about under some circumstances. The one carried curls up like a kitten, making a convenient bundle. When a colony decides to move its city, some of the ants select the new site, and commence carrying there not only the young and treasure but also their sister ants who are not alive to the necessity of removal. Sometimes the one seized upon in this summary fashion objects; but this in no-wise daunts the energetic mover, who hales her sister to the new home whether she will or no.

The older writers tell us of play spells among ants. During these times the inhabitants of an ant-hill indulge in wrestling games and gymnastics.

There are certain small insects which ants allow to dwell within their nests. So far as we can see, these guests are of no advantage to the ants, and it has been suggested that they are kept as pets. This is the only plausible theory to account for their presence in precincts where no intruders are tolerated.

Considering all the things we have discussed, and many other observed facts, for which there is no room in this brief sketch, it must be conceded that these insects are perfect socialists. We find that the individual is kind and self-sacrificing for its own commonwealth; and selfishness and cruelty and all the baser passions are aroused only in rivalry between communities. We find that the love of their kind is developed at the expense of all individual loves and hatreds. It is necessary that individual interests be subordinated in a perfect socialism; the communal instincts alone must vivify the individual. It may be claimed that these socialists are only insects, but the fact remains that they are the most intelligent creatures in this world that have, up to the present, made socialism a success.

It seems, then, from our study, that the most serious question that confronts our socialists of to-day is how to make man, in whom the individual instinct has grown strong through eons of development, conform to a plan in which the greatest success is attained only by the total effacement of individuality. It will surely require a large plan to include the greatest development of the individual and the utter levelling of social inequality — two tendencies that have ever pointed in diametrically opposite directions.

EPILOGUE : INDIVIDUALISM AS TAUGHT BY THE BEES

After studying the social development of these little creatures we are again reminded that when the course of evolution is set in one direction everything conduces to make that path the main road of progress and development. At first, and in the lower forms of life, it is the individual against the world. The next step is the union of two and the care of the young by one or both parents. Then it is the family against the world, the path of progress broadens so that at least two walk side by side. Then comes the forming of the individuals and families into societies, and many unite for the sake of protection or other advantage; and now the road is widened to admit many walking abreast; but they must press on shoulder to shoulder and the rear ranks perhaps in lock-step. The individual is no longer important except as he helps the whole; and any individual deviation from the beaten path is pronounced criminal by society and stamped out by evolution as a useless variation.

In the first and lower stage the individual is a perfect sphere, fully rounded in individuality. He owes nothing to the world; and utter selfishness is right for him because that is the path of his development. In the second stage the individual is no longer a perfect sphere but is flattened on two sides; he must sacrifice self for the sake of his mate and offspring. Then the social unit is composed of two or three cells, none of them perfectly rounded individuals; it is then two or three against the world. Then societies are formed and the organism is many celled; the individual is no longer rounded on any side; his rights are modified by the rights of every one around him; he now receives protection from the whole, and his individual development is modified by the laws that tend to the ultimate good of the whole ; only those individual traits are allowed to persist that are parallel with the direction of progress of the whole organism.

Great thinkers, philosophers, and poets, impatient of the restrictions that come from being one cell in a vast organism, have cried out for the divine right of a perfect self-development; many of our socialists and all of our anarchists are animated by this over-whelming longing for perfect self-rounding. But they forget that the monad is an anachronism in society ; the only possible chance for the human being to attain the perfect sphere of the individual is to retire to the desert and live a hermit. If he remains a part of the social organism and attempts to swell out the sphere of self to its pristine proportions, he is promptly secluded to four bare walls, where a well-rounded individuality does as little damage to others as possible; or, escaping this, he goes on fighting fate and disturbing the symme-try of the cells that press upon him for a little time, and is then thrown out by evolution as one of the great unfit.

All social struggles and revolutions of to-day come from the fact that the areas flattened by pressure of the several sides of the individual cells of the organism termed "society" are not yet settled and adjusted to the best advantage of the whole. We have only to wait to attain the perfect social mechanism of the bees.

Fig. 32.   Some Bush or Tree near a Stream.

V

TWO MOTHER MASONS

THESE are no female seekers after secrets of the masonic order, though they were free and accepted masons long before Solomon built his temple. They do not use the square and compass in their building because they do not need them. However, each of them has a pair of trowels which she uses with great dexterity. They are real ladies, too, these masons. There can be no doubt about it, for they have waists so slender and aristocratic that they would make the figures of a Parisian fashion-plate seem coarse in comparison. In fact, the waist in these masons is reduced to the size of a thread, and it seems almost impossible that the digestive organs can traverse so narrow a space and remain functional. This peculiarity gives the name to these masons of " Thread-waisted Wasps," for wasps they are. We must confess, however, physiologists to the contrary, that the slenderness of these " elegant figures " has no deleterious effect upon the health and strength of their owners. In fact there seems to be a distinct use for this extreme emaciation of the waist, for the abdomen is attached to it more or less like a knob; and if one of these wasps is carefully watched when flying, it is evident that the abdomen and long legs are carried in a manner to secure poise, and perhaps are also used in steering the insect in its strong, direct flight.

The first of these feminine masons for our consideration is *Sceliphron caementarius*, the "Cement Maker," popularly known as the "Mud Dauber." She is a graceful insect, with a shining black body and black wings that give off rainbow glints in the sunshine (Fig. 33). She is a most nervous and fidgety

FIG. 33. "A fidgety being."

being, and keeps her wings jerking when she is walking around, as if she had the St. Vitus' dance. Mayhap her nervousness comes from the burden of family cares; they all fall upon her, as her spouse is a short-lived, indolent fellow, who never dreams of lending her a helping mandible in the construction of the home.

It is safe to assert that in the insect world the question of "woman's rights" is settled permanently in the affirmative. With few exceptions the insect husband and father is a care-free, irresponsible individual, who gives no consideration to the sheltering or feeding of his family. On the other hand, many insect mothers wear themselves out in unselfish toil in caring for their young. Both of our lady masons ply their trade solely for the housing of their offspring.

The Cement Maker is well named. We find her in early summer very busy at the edges of pools and in other damp places collecting mud; this she mixes with saliva into a strong mortar by means of her trowel jaws. This mortar she uses to build the mud houses, with which we who dwell in country places are so familiar. They are constructed beneath the rafters and roof boards of barns and sheds, or any building where the wasp can gain access, and consist of two or more parallel tubes about an inch long. On the inside the tubes are smooth and regular, but the outside of the structure is rough and rude, with no architectural pretensions. That this wasp knows how to make a very adhesive cement those of us can attest who have tried to remove all traces of one of her dwellings. She is in the habit of consulting her own convenience rather than ours in choosing sites for her houses. One year she or one of her relatives plastered up all the keyholes in one of our bureaus so effectually that the locks were afterward useless. Another utilized a sand hole in the side of a flat-iron, little dreaming what would happen

to her progeny next ironing day. Another found the
telephone a convenient place for locating a house ; and
a few years since one species of the Cement Makers
acquired the habit of building in the ends of the air-
brake tubes of the cars on one of the western railroads.
The management, frightened by visions of inevitable
collisions, sought counsel of experts. " Make a slit
opening to the tube," was the efficacious advice of the
entomologist.

After the Cement Maker has finished her first tube
she leaves one end open and flies off in quest of her
prey. Now the wasp is not a vegetarian like the bee,
and she has before her the duty of supplying her young
with meat rather than bread. As her eggs are laid in
hot weather, and as enough food must be stored in the
cell with the egg to mature the larva, the question is
how to preserve meat fresh for so long a time. She
meets the difficulty thus : she hunts for spiders and
when she finds one she pounces upon it, stings it, and carries it to the mud cell and places it within. She repeats
this process until she has placed as many spiders in the
tube as, according to her judgment, will be needed. She
then lays an egg in the cell and walls up the opening.

The remarkable thing about this performance is the
magical effect of her sting. Whether it is the result
of a subtle poison or whether it is the special spot in

the spider's nervous system where the sting is inserted we do not know; certain it is that after being thus stung it lives on in a paralyzed condition for weeks and even months. It can move but slightly and remains helpless in its mud prison until the wasp egg hatches into a voracious grub which at once falls to and eats with great relish the meat thus miraculously preserved.

One observation made by Walcknaer upon a mason wasp that provisions her nest with bees, seems to indicate that, in one case at least, the place selected for stinging caused the paralysis. He says, "The wasp pounces upon the bee, seizes it by the back, and placing it by the side of a small stone or pile of earth she turns it around upon its back, then standing on its body in an attitude of conscious triumph she darts her sting into the lower part of the head in such a manner as to stupefy but not to kill it outright."

Whether the sting renders the spider insensible to pain or not is a question that only the spider could answer. However, it is probable that it does. Anyway we need waste no sympathy on the spider, the most bloodthirsty of all the "little people" of the field and woods. There is indeed a sense of retributive justice in the thought of a spider helpless and at the mercy of a small creature which it would have ruthlessly devoured had it been able.

So we should not accuse our Cement Maker of any unreasonable cruelty, if she, like us, insists upon a nitrogenous diet for her young. Nor need we have any fear of her sting, as she seldom uses it as a weapon of offence or defence; in any case the pain occasioned by her sting is trivial. The Cement Maker is really one of the most harmless and one of the most interesting of the summer visitors to our window-panes.

The other mother mason is *Eumenes fraterna*, the Jug Builder. In appearance she is far more gay than the Cement Maker, the dark bronze of her graceful body being ornamented with yellow bars and spots. Her æsthetic sense is also better developed than is that of her black cousin, and she is also a more clever artisan. However, in the matter of strength and durability, the Cement Maker's structures are superior.

Some fine morning in early spring the Jug Builder selects some twig of bush or tree that is conveniently near the banks of a brook or pond and on this begins to construct her nest. Her building material consists of sand or gravel which she cements together with mud mixed with saliva. This cement is similar to that of the Mud Dauber; but the latter constructs her nest entirely of cement while the Jug Builder is a stone layer as well as a plasterer. The Jug Builder's walls when examined with a lens look like the walls of a cobblestone

house laid with more mortar than cobblestones. It is
interesting to note that this small mason understands
the value of hair as a strengthening ingredient in her
mortar and so uses every stray hair she can find. She
makes her walls in layers and is most careful to preserve the symmetry of her building as she proceeds.

When finished,
the nest is
globular in
shape, with an
opening at the
top that flares
gracefully at
the rim ; the
whole looks
very much like
a minute olla
or Mexican

FIG. 34.   The Jug Builder and her Nests.

water jug. While this little cobblestone dwelling is
necessarily somewhat rough outside it is very smooth
inside and apparently silk lined. Just how the wasp
makes this lining we do not know, for the adult wasp is
supposed to have no means of spinning silk. Some entomologists have suggested that the larva lines the nest,
but no one who has examined with a lens the walls of
this little dwelling could but believe that the smooth

fibrous lining was a part of the original construction. Perhaps the wasp covers the inner walls with a saliva that in drying splits into silklike fibres. However, if the *Eumenes* suspend the egg as Fabre declares, they must have some means of spinning silk.

When the nest is finished as described, the mother mason turns hunter, and caterpillars are her quarry. She stings them as she catches them, as did the Mud Dauber the spiders; however, the Jug Builder does not seem to have so powerful a weapon, for the caterpillars are imperfectly paralyzed. They are still able to wriggle in a quite disconcerting manner after she has dumped them down through the opening into the jug. After she has secured a sufficient number of these to sustain her young until it has reached maturity she lays an egg and fastens it to the dome of the nest; this is, perhaps, the reason that the opening to the jug is always a little at the side. After the egg is laid she closes the opening by filling it with a cork of cement.

The story of what goes on in the *Eumenes*' nest after the mother has walled up the cell has been told with great vivacity and most dramatically by the French entomologist, J.-H. Fabre. He made little windows in the sides of the jugs, and so was able to see what had always before been shrouded in mystery and darkness. He says : —

"The egg is not deposited on the food; it is suspended from the summit of the dome by a thread which rivals in fineness that of the web of the spider. At the least breath the delicate cylinder trembles, oscillates; it recalls to me the famous pendulum attached to the cupola of the Pantheon in order to demonstrate the rotation of the earth. The food is heaped below.

"Second act of this marvellous spectacle: in order to look on, let us open a window in cells until fortune smiles on us. The larva is hatched and is already growing up. Like the egg, it is suspended vertically a little way from the floor of the dwelling; but the suspending thread has notably increased in length and is composed of the first thread to which is added a sort of a ribbon. The larva is at table; with lowered head it is burrowing in the flabby body of one of the caterpillars. With the tip of a straw I touched lightly the game as yet intact. The caterpillars squirmed. Instantly the larva retired from the mêlée. And how? Marvel upon marvel! That which I had taken for a flat band, for a ribbon at the lower end of the suspending thread, is a sheath, a robe, a tube of ascension, in which the larva crept up backwards. The cast skin of the egg-shell, preserved cylindrical and prolonged perchance by a special work of the newly hatched larva, forms this channel of refuge. At the least sign of peril in the heap of caterpillars, the larva retreats into its sheath and climbs to the roof, where the writhing mob cannot reach it. When quiet is restored, it creeps down its tube and commences eating again, with head lowered upon the food and the abdomen aloft ready for retreat upward.

"Third and last act: strength has been attained; the larva is sufficiently vigorous to be no longer afraid of the movements of the heap of caterpillars. They, on the other hand, eaten into by the larva, attenuated by the long torpor, are less able to defend themselves. The perils of the tender newly born are succeeded by the security of robust adolescence; and the larva disdaining thereafter its ascension sheath lets itself down on its remaining food. Thus it banquets afterwards in the ordinary manner of its family."

Our emotions upon reading these revelations of the drama that takes place in the *Eumenes'* cell depend upon whether our sympathies are with the wasp or the caterpillars. However, in studying the histories of animals, we had best start out with the cheerful theory that a "square meal" is due to any creature that is strong enough or cunning enough to get it; and that it is a futile waste of sensibilities to sympathize with the meal.

To return to our mother builder : her work is by
no means done when she has finished one house, for
she builds several.   She sometimes places three or four
together along one twig ; sometimes she seems to get
tired, and we find two neighboring jugs, one much
smaller than the other.   Late in summer we find
these jugs with holes in their sides, showing where
the adults have made their escape from the dark, safe
homes.   But whenever we find these cunning little
structures we always pause to admire them and yield
our tribute of praise to the clever mother mason that
built them.

Fig. 35.   "A raspberry bramble, low trailing and graceful."

VI

THE STORY WE LOVE BEST

A BRANCH of sumac with its drum-
major plumes, a bough of elder
bending under its load of dark-
hued berries, a raspberry bramble,
low trailing and graceful; these
were my trophies from woodland
one sunny October afternoon, and to the uninitiated they
doubtless would seem but random and commonplace
mementos of an autumn ramble. But these branches,
seemingly uninteresting and aimlessly gathered, have
been the scenes of great toil, brave deeds, faithful devotion, and also, alas, of treachery and tragedy. I will
relate to you the history revealed by these broken
boughs — a history to discover which has required
many patient hours of watching by eyes that loved
the work.

One morning last May, had you been watching, you
might have seen a little insect, not more than a fourth
of an inch long flitting about these branches, her body
metallic blue, and her four gauzy wings flashing in the

sunlight. Had you noted her then, you would have
thought her created only for the enjoyment of a bright
spring day. Little would you have dreamed of the
strength of purpose and the power of endurance bound
up in that wee body. You perhaps would have scarcely
detected that she belonged to a family noted for perse-
verance and industry. Yet, despite her diminutive size,
and metallic colors, she is as truly a bee as the clumsiest
bumblebee that ever hummed in the clover. She
belongs especially, however, to the group of carpenter
bees; she has a pretty scientific name, *Ceratina dupla*,
that seems quite in keeping with her dainty personality.
Her popular name is simply the " Little Carpenter Bee."

However, very little cares she by what Latin name
mortal man has chosen to call her, for weighty responsi-
bilities rest upon her mind this bright May morning;
and so she hunts until she finds some broken twig of
elder or sumac which permits her to come into direct
contact with the pith of the plant. Then our heroine,
with the aid of her mandibles or jaws, commences to
excavate a tunnel in the branch by removing the pith
mouthful by mouthful. Very carefully is the work
done, the pith being neatly cut, so that the walls of the
tunnel are left straight and smooth. To bring her
undertaking within our comprehension we might compare
her to a man who should attempt to dig a well three or

four feet wide and two hundred feet deep, and with no tools except his hands with which to remove the earth.

The tunnel of the *Ceratina* is about one-eighth of an inch in diameter, and often as much as eight or ten inches in depth. But when our little bee is through excavating her tunnel and has finished it with all the nicety prompted by her own fine sense of the fitness of things, she has really but begun her summer's work. Her next task combines pleasure and duty, for it takes her into the fields to gather pollen from the flowers. This she carries little by little to the tunnel; but it requires many trips back and forth before she has packed the bottom of the nest with pollen to the depth of a quarter of an inch. This done she deposits upon it a tiny white egg; and then she proceeds to build a partition above by gluing together bits of pith and other suitable material with a glue which she always keeps on hand, or rather in mouth, for the purpose. This partition is fastened firmly to the sides of the tunnel and is about one-tenth of an inch thick; it serves as a roof for the first cell and as a floor for the next. Then the process is repeated; she gathers more pollen, lays another egg, builds another partition, and so on, until the tunnel is filled to within an inch or so of the opening; the last egg is thus necessarily deposited many days after the first one.

Thus, you see, this matron has her family in an apartment house, each child occupying an entire flat (Fig. 36). Then there comes a time of rest for the industrious little mother; for her next duty is to remain quiet and wait for her family to grow up. But her fidelity is unfailing; the space left empty at the top of the tunnel serves as a vestibule to her dwelling, and there she waits and watches over her home.

While she is guarding the door let us take a peep into the

Fig. 36.   Little Carpenter Bee and her Nest.

first cell and see what is taking place there. From the egg there hatches a minute, white, footless larva which immediately falls to eating the pollen provided by its thoughtful mother. On this food it thrives and grows, until it is a quarter of an inch long; by this

time, probably, it has consumed all the pollen in the
cell ; however the mother bee's instinct does not seem to
be infallible in this particular, for sometimes she provides
more food than her offspring needs.   After the larva has
thus reached its full growth, it becomes rigid and turns
darker in color, and queer-looking seams and excres-
cences appear upon it ; these are the cases in which its
legs and wings are developing; in short, it becomes a
pupa.   After remaining in this state some time the pupa
skin bursts open, and a full-fledged bee appears, resem-
bling its mother in size, color, and general aspect.
Meanwhile, the patient mother, who has not shared our
privilege of peeping into the cells, knows nothing of
what has happened therein, unless, perchance, she
remembers her own larvahood.   Her experience is a
novel one, for her first-born is the last one of the brood
that she beholds.   Patience is taught to these creatures
as an early lesson ; for, of course, the bee that hatches
from the first-laid egg reaches maturity soonest.   So
the first experience of the eldest of the *Ceratina* family
is to wait until its younger brothers and sisters above
it have grown up.   We may imagine that this idle
waiting is rather tedious to a little creature with
brand new wings which it is longing to spread in the
sunshine.

The next lesson that our young *Ceratina* must learn

is to work. For, when the youngest of the brood has
reached maturity, each one in the nest begins to work
its way upward toward the door by tearing down the
partition above it and pushing the particles of waste
material down toward the bottom of the nest. This arrangement is a very comfortable one for the youngest,
which has only one partition between him and his
mother. But it is not nearly so pleasant for the eldest,
which had not only the longest time to wait but now
has most work to do; for he must push his way up
through the débris of all the partitions above him.
It reveals a funny sight to open a *Ceratina* nest after
the material of the partitions has all been stowed away
in the bottom of the tunnel. There are all the bees —
sometimes as many as fourteen — packed in as closely
as possible, each with its head toward the opening, and
braced against the heels, so to speak, of its next
younger brother; for nature teaches them to face
toward the door that leads out into the world. Finally,
the sentinel mother, having become satisfied that all
are ready, leads her children in their first flight in the
sunshine.

Later the remains of the partitions are removed,
and the nest is thus made ready for another brood.
Sometimes the whole grown-up family is found in a
nest thus cleaned, which would indicate that the young

bees dutifully lend their mother a helping mandible in house cleaning and in making the home attractive. And they doubtless find it pleasant to linger about the old homestead and make it their abiding-place until they feel capable of setting up establishments of their own. This is certainly true of the fall brood. These children of the autumn, when the days become cool, crawl into the clean nest, head downward, one after another, and tuck themselves in as cosy as cosy can be, and just go to sleep and stay asleep until the bright May sunshine calls to them through the open door and tells them to wake up and go to work. I have often wondered if this long winter's sleep were not brightened by dreams of sunlight and flowers. How do we know that this is not the bee's way of spending the winter in Florida?

Thus we have learned the main facts in the life of our little *Ceratina,* supposing that her life has been fortunate from egg to motherhood. But in our studies of these hidden homes we find records of struggles and tragedies and thus learn that our tiny friend has many enemies always watching for an opportunity to injure her and hers. Among these foes are some of her own depraved and lazy relatives who certainly ought to have better manners and morals. Other species of bees, and some wasps, which build their nests in the hollow stalks of plants, take advantage of the tunnel excavated by *Ceratina*, and drive her away before her nest is finished and take possession of her home. We may safely believe that the plucky little bee would not submit to such an outrage without vigorous remonstrance; and doubtless on such occasions there are duels fought which equal in bravery and ferocity any fought by Knights Errant of old.

There are still other enemies of the *Ceratina* too mean and cowardly to achieve their objects by fair fight. One of these, a light and airy insect, with cimeter-shaped body, belongs to the *Ichneumonidæ*, a family noted for deceitfulness, treachery, and bloodthirstiness. This designing creature loiters about and watches the *Ceratina* building her nest. When the busy builder has filled a cell with pollen, and laid an egg upon it, and has departed to seek materials for a partition, the ichneumon sneaks in and lays one of her eggs there, too; so when the bee comes back she unconsciously walls in with her child its deadliest foe. When the young bee is nearly grown, the ichneumon egg hatches into a voracious little grub, which evidently looks upon the fat bee-larva as choice beefsteak. It falls at once to eating the helpless creature, which conveniently yields sufficient food to nourish the interloper until it completes its growth. Then the ichneumon spins a beautiful silken cocoon about itself and with calm effrontery changes to a pupa. In this state it waits until the bees above it have matured and departed, and then it issues, a full-fledged ichneumon, and flies out into the world to perpetuate the hereditary tricks of its family. We found one of these ichneumon cocoons in the middle cell of a *Ceratina* nest. Only one of the mature bees was found in the tunnel below the cocoon, and it had its head pointed downward, thus telling, as plainly as words could have told, that, disgusted with the creature it found obstructing its upward pathway, it had turned about with a firm intention to dig out by way of China, if necessary. Undoubtedly, many bees, which escape being eaten by the parasite, die thus from imprisonment.

This completes the record of all we discovered during one summer about the *Ceratina*. It is difficult to express in mere words how this beautiful little creature won our hearts. Just the sight of her has always been a joy to us since; to us she is something more than a mere creature of instinct; she is a bee of character. Our last glimpse of her was in November, when we found a family of eight in a clean nest, one behind the other, head downward, packed away snugly for the winter. The bee in the most exposed position next to the door — the bee last to seek shelter after all the others were safely housed — was the faithful little mother. We knew her because her wings were frayed and worn by her many flights and severe toil. In vain would the voices of the coming May call her to a life of sunshine and blue sky, for her poor wings could carry her but a little way, and she would never again gather the pollen from willing flowers. But there she was, still on guard, still yielding the last energies of her ebbing life in unselfish devotion to her home and family.

Fig. 37.   A Basswood Tree.

VII

A DWELLER IN TENTS

NEAR one of my favorite woodland paths stands a young basswood tree. Every summer, during the months of July and August, this tree presents a very strange and, if truth be told, a decidedly dishevelled appearance. At first glance it would seem as though each individual leaf had become dissatisfied with its form and had concluded to remodel itself according to its own caprice. Close inspection reveals but few leaves on the entire tree that retain their normal shape; and what is true of this tree is, I fear, true of many basswood trees each summer throughout the northern United States.

The cause of this ragged appearance of these handsome trees is, however, not to be attributed to rebellion and anarchy on the part of the leaves. The real agent is a lively little "worm," which cuts the leaf half across and makes the flap into a roll, wherein he lives and feeds, safe from the sharp eyes of hungry birds and from the vicissitudes of rain and wind.

This little householder has no doorplate to announce his name to the world; possibly because his house would afford scant room for the dignified name *Pantographa limata*. From this omission on his part to vaunt his real name he is commonly called the " Basswood Leaf-roller," that being our rather crude way of distinguishing his caterpillarship from others of his kind which take possession of our forests in happy summer time.

FIG. 38.   A Basswood Leaf rolled into Tents.

One August day I plucked one of these rolled leaves with the intent of studying the inmate (Fig. 38). I found the little tent-ropes of silk that fastened the roll down to the leaf were quite strong, requiring conscious effort to tear them asunder as I made my way into the green tube. It was not until the leaf was entirely unrolled that I discovered the tenant. He was a handsome little creature according to caterpillar standards of beauty (Fig. 39); his green body had an opalescent sheen that was most gemlike; and his head and thorax were vividly, aggressively black and shining. Notwith-

standing my admiring glances he was not at all pleased
to make my acquaintance and evinced his displeasure
by twisting and wriggling most spitefully. He hurried
this way and that, never taking the trouble to turn
around, for he was quite as adept in " backing " as he
was in going forward.

Finally he buried his head under a corner of the
leaf and remained motionless. Evidently the beautiful
philosophy of the ostrich was his also.
However, he was soon made aware of the
fallacy of this reasoning, for I proceeded to
examine him in detail through my lens. I
noted the shining tubercles, six on each
segment, as seen from above, four in front
and two behind, each one adorned with a
bristle. I noted the alertness of the highly
polished black head and the thoracic shield
shining like ebony. I was interested to find that his
six true feet were apparently encased in patent
leathers, after the most approved and latest fashion in
gentlemen's boots.

Fig. 39. The
Tent-dweller.

I found him so interesting that I rolled him up in
his leaf and took him home and placed him in a
box, intending to sketch him very soon. Alas, must
I confess it ? That very day I began a new and
absorbing piece of work that crowded out all thoughts

not relating to it, and I forgot all about my little leaf-roller for a week. I suddenly remembered him with a pang of remorse and hastened to him. I fully expected to find my prisoner a wasted corpse. But no! he had fastened his broken tent down again with silken ropes; then, finding the pasturage getting dry, had abandoned his old home and folded over and fastened a corner of the leaf, in vain hope of finding there fresher food. In this lesser tent I found him a little pale, it is true, but with spirit still un-daunted. He greeted me with a spiteful jerk; this time his scornful rejection of my advances seemed justi-fied. I sent immediately for fresh leaves and trans-ferred him to one of them. In a very short time he had folded an edge of the leaf over himself and secured it with a web of silk. But he had concluded, evidently, that eating was not a safe indulgence in this uncertain world, for he refused to take even a nibble from his new pasture. It may be, however, that he had so far matured that he no longer needed food; possibly he was ready to seek a nook under leaves or earth in which to spend the winter, and was meditating upon the fact that the hand of fate which swept him from his native tree had placed him beyond the reach of earth in which to hide.

I first made a full-length portrait of him; a per-

formance on my part which he manifestly regarded as
an unpardonable liberty. I then made a detailed study
of the head and thorax (Fig. 40).
To do this I placed him in a watch-
glass, while I studied him through
a compound microscope. While I
looked he lifted his second booted

leg in a deprecating way as if to
say, "Is there then in this wide
world no justice to be meted out to

Fig. 40.   Head and Two
Thoracic Segments of the
Caterpillar of *P. limata.*

mortals who outrage the rights and persons of innocent
caterpillars ? "

I tried to put on paper this deprecatory attitude, but
it was too subtle for my clumsy powers of delineation.
In fact, he was from first to last a very bad "sitter" and
very exhausting to the artist's patience. However, he
was well worth the trouble he cost, for he was as interesting as a harlequin in his vivid costume of black and
green. The black face was made grotesque by ten
little eyes of assorted sizes, placed in circles, each one
shining like an opal. His black legs were adorned at
the joints with what a costumer would call " slashes "
that revealed a lining of green ; on the segment nearest
the body the black band was cut into gay points.

When I finished the sketch I rolled him in his
leaf and took him out into the woods. Then, asking

his pardon for inconveniencing him, wishing him a comfortable winter, a successful pupahood in the spring, and a final glorification into mothhood in June, I placed him under his own basswood tree.

Fig. 41.   Moth of the Basswood Leaf-roller.

The adult of *Pantographa limata* is a very pretty moth, with wings of delicate buff marked with olive-green. There is a beautiful purplish iridescence to the olive-green, which is a delight to the eye that loves delicate, suggestive color.

The interesting thing about this species from a scientific standpoint is that it has broken away from family traditions and become a leaf-roller. Most of the leaf-rolling caterpillars belong to the *Tortricina*, although rarely they are found in other families. Our little friend belongs to the *Pyralidina*, and has developed his leaf-rolling habit entirely independent of his ancestors or near relatives. If the individual which I studied fairly represents the species, I am not surprised at this original line of development; for in all my dealing with insect kind I have never met one of the "little brothers" who knew his own mind more clearly and conclusively than the subject of this sketch.

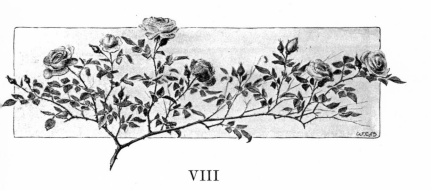

VIII

A TACTFUL MOTHER

EVERYWHERE in the world the wisest mothers are those who do all in their power to make their children good. The most successful method of doing this, I suppose, is to make it easier for children to be good than to be bad, by removing the sources of temptations to naughtiness. The little mother of this story has a wonderful device of this sort by which she controls her naturally selfish and greedy family.

This mother is a pretty, tiny creature, dainty enough to belong to the court of a fairy queen. She has green wings about a half inch in length, and all through them runs a network of darker green veins. No lady ever dressed for a ball in a prettier combination of gauze and lace than this little creature wears every day. Her slender body is also pale green, and her antennæ are brown; but her greatest beauty lies in a pair of large eyes that shine and glow like liquid gold. As much praise cannot be given to the perfume she affects as to her personal appearance; many a person who has captured this delicate creature has been surprised at the disagreeable odor she exhaled. However, the very purpose of this questionable perfume is to discourage obtrusive people and birds from becoming too familiar with her. Because of her beauty she has been called "Lace-wing" and "Golden-Eyes" by her admirers, but her scientific name is *Chrysopa*, and her family is called the *Chrysopidæ*.

We might naturally infer that such a lovely mother would have most attractive children, but this is far from true. The young of Madam Lace-wing are short-legged, spindle-shaped, sturdy little fellows, with no signs of wings but with great sickle-shaped jaws. Now the form of insect jaws is the unfailing index of insect character; when they are sharp pointed and huge, as in this case, they mean death and destruction to any smaller insect unfortunate enough to cross the path of their owner. The more common prey of the young *Chrysopa* are the aphids or plant-lice; so destructive to the aphis are these bloodthirsty creatures that they are known as aphis-lions. Although we may not look with pleasure on such wholesale slaughter, yet we must confess that we owe the aphis-lions a vote of thanks for

Fig. 42.   Lace-wing Fly, her Eggs, Larva, and Cocoon.

their work in destroying plant-lice which infest almost every plant and tree that we try to cultivate and which are the inveterate foes of our roses.

However, there is little virtue in the intentions of the aphis-lion. His highest aspiration is to find something that he may eat; and not alone aphids but every insect egg that he finds and every insect that he can conquer helps to fill his insatiable little stomach. His method of killing his prey is peculiar. Each of his sickle-shaped jaws is composed of a mandible, with a groove along its entire length and a maxilla fitting over this groove, so as to make a tube one end of which opens at the tip of the jaw and the other opening in the creature's mouth. When he catches an aphid, he thrusts these long, hollow weapons into its soft body and lifts it high in the air, as if drinking a bumper, while he sucks its blood through his tubular jaws as a man would drink lemonade through two straws.

Now we come to the problem that the mother Lacewing had to solve : If she merely laid her eggs on the leaf in a group, the earliest hatched larva, in hunting for something to satisfy his first hunger, would surely turn cannibal and make his first meal off his unhatched brothers and sisters. Little mother Golden-eyes is not so frivolous and silly as her transparent beauty might suggest. She has wisdom to solve her perplexing problem satisfactorily, and this is her method : When about to lay an egg she places first a minute drop of sticky fluid on the surface of the leaf; this she spins up into a slender thread by lifting it on the tip of her abdomen as high as she can; the air dries the thread quickly, and it is strong enough to sustain the egg which she fastens on top of it. The result is that each egg is supported a half inch above the surface of the leaf by a hair-like pedicel. These groups of *Chrysopa* eggs are very pretty and are often mistaken for patches of glistening white fungus upon leaves, for they look more like the spore cases of fungi than like eggs.

When the eldest of the family breaks his shell, he drops or scrambles down from his egg perch as best he can, and in his immediate hunt for food wanders harmlessly around the bases of the threads which support his unhatched brothers and sisters far above his head and probably beyond his sight. His rapid-moving little legs take him soon far from his birthplace to where unsuspecting aphids are pumping sap, and then the slaughter begins unless, perchance, some ant guardian averts the attack. Each member of the family in its turn follows his example and wanders out into the great world beyond its native leaf, guiltless of fratricide. Yet if two aphis-lions meet there is likely to be a trial of strength. I saw one once try to drink the family blood flowing in a younger brother's body; he attempted at first to find a weak place in the armor of his intended victim, but the latter always turned and twisted in a way to present a horny surface to his murderous brother and thus managed finally to escape, though he certainly showed evidences of genuine fright.

After a season of larval imbibing each aphis-lion rolls itself up in a little ball and weaves around itself a thick coat of glistening white silk, thus making a cocoon that looks like a seed-pearl fastened to a leaf. It is to be hoped that during this period of voluntary seclusion the recluse meditates upon the selfishness of its past career and decides upon an entire reformation. This is evidently the case; for, after a time, perhaps a whole winter, it cuts a dainty, circular lid at the top of its pearl-prison and emerges a creature no longer spindle shaped and sickle jawed, but with wide, filmy wings that have been folded and packed in the tiny cocoon. In fact, the wonders which have been worked in that pearly cell are greater than those wrought by any magician in fairy tale; for within its walls an ugly, greedy aphis-lion has been changed to a beautiful, golden-eyed lace-wing.

After studying this *Chrysopa* biography, one naturally wonders how these golden-eyed mothers gained so much wisdom; how did they happen to think out such a fine scheme? Scientists will answer that it was not thought out at all, but has been brought about by a certain fairy godmother called "Evolution." They say that long, long ago the *Chrysopa* ancestresses merely fastened their eggs to the leaf with a drop of sticky fluid; and probably only a few of the young escaped the fate of filling fraternal stomachs. But there were some mothers which happened to secrete larger drops or raised them by accident a little higher from the surface of the leaf, and thus saved more of their children from the cannibalistic attacks of the first-born; and these offspring inherited this saving tendency to place their eggs on pedicels. Thus, little by little, the habit has been developed until we have a family, *Chrysopidæ*, that lays eggs upon stalks, while all the *Chrysopidæ* that knew no better than to lay their eggs on the surface of the leaf were exterminated long ago through their own foolishness and lack of foresight.

This is what evolutionists would say; and they would also assure us that all insects perform all their wise acts through inherited habit instead of through wise thinking. However, I think it is a prettier theory to believe that mother Lace-wing lays her eggs on stalks just because she wishes her children to be good, and so "leads them not into temptation."

Fig. 43.   The Haunts of the " Water-sprite."

IX

HERE is a certain stream I know that begins as a brook, traversing a high meadow sweet with clover and white with daisies. It then forsakes sunny heights and glides down a pine-covered hill, where great roots interlace and hold firm its banks; thence it tumbles down a slope beset with birch and sumac, and finally, under some furry young hemlocks that protect it from an "attacking army of rainbows," it takes a wild plunge to wider levels below.

This brook, fed from living springs, is the theatre of myriad life, and it was

"Down the golden-braided centre of its current swift and strong,"

that I first saw a quaint little fisherman that spreads his nets for fry too small for our coarse eyes to see, but which, nevertheless, prove all-sufficient for his needs. Well is he named *Hydropsyche*, "the water-sprite."

133

Most skilfully he makes his snare.   It is formed like a dip-net and fastened with silk to a frame of leaves

or pebbles, so that its distended mouth is directed up-stream. Near the frame it consists of fragments of vegetation woven into a silken tapestry and is finished at the end with a bag

Fig. 44. A Seine and the Fisherman's Hut.

of coarse, even mesh.   The regularity of this bit of netting is beautiful to behold, and its use shows the cleverness of the builder.   This large mesh allows the water to flow through freely, and thereby leave entangled in the seine any little creature not small enough to pass through.   The mechanism of the structure is simple and self regulating.

On the side of this tiny seine toward the current of the stream is a little passage which leads to the seine-builder's house.   This is a rather crudely constructed tube made of sticks and stones fastened to the surface of the stone with silk, and just large enough to fit its occupant.   Lying in his house, his alert head reaching out in the passageway, our small fisherman needs only to take a step or two to examine his haul and sate his appetite.

This clever little artisan is a caterpillar hardly more

Fig. 45. The Wider Levels.

than a half inch in length when fully grown.   In color
he is brownish or olive-green, and has three pairs of
true legs, which are longer than the legs usually vouch-
safed to caterpillars.   He has black eyes which give
him a keen, alert expression of countenance when seen
through a lens.   Along the lower surface of his body
are tiny tassels of thread, which are his tracheal gills
and enable him to breathe the oxygen mixed with the
swift-flowing water, so he does not have to rise to the
surface to take breath.   His body bears at the rear end
a pair of stout hooks.   It is by means of these that he
grasps his silken ropes and is not swept away down-
stream by the swift current.   He loves to spread his
nets on the very brink of waterfalls, and there they
remain long after he has abandoned them, making the
rock dark with the refuse caught in their cunning
meshes.

When the fisherman has found in his nets, day after
day, sufficient sustenance to complete his growth he asks
no more of the kindly waters but retires to his shabby
house, patches it up, mayhap, making it stronger and
more torrent-proof; and he builds a grating of silk at
either end which allows the water to pass through
freely, bringing oxygen for breathing, but carefully
excludes small enemies that might find their way in
through an unbarred door.   Thus protected, he changes

to a pupa. After a time he bursts the pupa skin, tears down the bars at the door, and shoots like an arrow to the surface of the stream. In this upward course he swims with his long legs and holds his wings folded tightly upon his back. The instant he reaches the surface the wings unfold like magic and bear him away into a new and unknown medium.

No more fundamental change of habit can be imagined. This creature that has lived his whole life beneath the surface of the water, clinging to perilous brinks with his anchoring hooks, making and spreading his nets on slippery, submerged rocks, suddenly in a second changes to a true denizen of the air. For this he is now equipped with soft, brown, leathery wings, folded roof-like over his back ; and with long thread-like antennæ that continually touch all things within their reach with delicate inquisitiveness; and with long, slender legs, stockinged in ornate hairs of which any moth might be justly proud.

His life in the air is short and sweet. Hiding himself during the garish day he comes out in the shadowy night and seeks his mate. She may have been his nearest neighbor at the bottom of the stream, but she was nothing to him then. Now she is all there is of life's happiness. As soon as he, after brief possession, loses her, he seems to realize there is naught else worth living for, and he dashes toward the first light that affords him opportunity for self-immolation. Does he perchance regard it as some near star, whereon he may find another incarnation ? With dazzled eyes he flings himself into it and speedily experiences the ecstasy of martyrdom, yielding with mad joy his body and delicate wings to brighten for one instant the sacrificial flame.

Fɪɢ. 46.   The Home Tree of Little Hermit Brother.

X

HERMIT AND TROUBADOUR

A JUNE STORY FOR JUNIOR NATURALISTS

IN far Thibet exists a class of Buddhist monks who are hermits and who dwell in caves. I was told about these strange people by a senior naturalist, who has spent his life going around the world and finding the countries upon it as easily as you junior naturalists find the same countries on the globe in the schoolroom. A real naturalist is never contented with maps of places and pictures of things, but always desires to see the places and things themselves.

The senior naturalist told me that he found Thibet a dreary land inhabited by queer people; and the hermit monks were the queerest of all. Each one dwelt in his solitary cave, ate very little, and worked not at all, but spent his time in thought. Could we read his thoughts we would be none the wiser, since they are only mysterious thoughts about mysterious things.

Now it is a surprising fact that we have hermits of similar habits in America; only our hermits are a little people who dress in white garb and live in cells underground; they also eat little and work not at all and probably meditate upon mysteries. However, they are equipped with six legs, while the monks of Thibet have only two — a difference of little importance, since none of them travel far from their caves.

In order that you may know the mysterious lives of these American hermits, I will relate to you the history of one of them.

Seventeen years ago this June, when perhaps the parents of some of the junior naturalists were themselves school children, a cicada mother made with her ovipositor a little slit or cavity in an elm twig, and in this slit placed in very neat order two rows of eggs. Six weeks later there hatched from one of these eggs a pale, lively, little creature, that to the naked eye looked like a tiny white ant. However, if we could have examined him through a lens, we would have found him very different from an ant; for his two front legs were shaped somewhat like lobsters' big claws, and instead of jaws like an ant's he simply had a long beak

that was hollow like a tube. After he came out of his
egg he ran about the tree and seemed interested in
everything he saw for a time. Then, suddenly, he went
to the side of a limb and deliberately fell off. To his
little eyes the ground below was invisible ; so our
small cicada showed great faith when he practically
jumped off the edge of his world into space. He was
such a speck of a creature that the breeze took him and
lifted him gently down, as if he were the petal of a
flower, and he alighted on the earth unhurt and probably
much delighted with his sail through the air. At once
he commenced hunting for some little crevice in the
earth; and when he found it he went to the bottom
of it and with his shovel-like forefeet began digging
downward. I wonder if he stopped to give a last look
at sky, sunshine, and the beautiful green world before
he bade them good-by for seventeen long years. If so,
he did it hurriedly, for he was intent upon reaching
something to eat. This he finally found a short distance below the surface of the ground in the shape of
a juicy rootlet of the great tree above. Into this he
inserted his beak and began to take the sap as we take
lemonade through a straw. He made a little cell
around himself, and then he found existence quite bliss-
ful. He ate very little and grew very slowly, and
there was no perceptible change in him for about a

year; then he shed his skin for the first time and thus, insect-wise, grew larger. After a time he dug another cell near another rootlet deeper in the ground; but he never exerted himself more than was necessary to obtain the little food that he needed. This idle life he found entirely satisfactory, and the days grew into months and the months into years. Only six times in the seventeen years did our hermit change his clothes; and this was each time a necessity, since they had become too small. Judging from what the senior naturalist told me, I think this is six times more than a Thibetan hermit changes his clothes in the same length of time.

What may be the meditations of a little hermit cicada during all these years we cannot even imagine. If any of the junior naturalists ever find out the secret, they will be very popular indeed with the scientific men called psychologists. However, if we may judge by actions, the sixteenth summer after our hermit buried himself he began to feel stirring in his bosom aspirations toward a higher life. He surely had no memory of the beautiful world he had abandoned in his babyhood, but he became suddenly possessed with a desire to climb upward and began digging his way toward the light. It might prove a long journey through the hard earth; for during the many years he may have reached the depth

of nearly two feet.   He is now as industrious as he was
shiftless before, and it takes him only a few weeks to
climb out of the depths into which he had fallen
through nearly seventeen years of inertia.   If it should
chance that he reaches the surface of the ground before
he is ready to enjoy life, he hits upon a device for con-
tinuing his way upward without danger to himself.
Sometimes his fellows have been known to crawl out of
their burrows and seek safety under logs and stakes
until the time came to gain their wings.   But this is a
very dangerous proceeding, since there are many watch-
ful eyes in forests which belong to creatures who are
very fond of bits of soft white meat.   So our cicada, still
a hermit, may build him a tall cell out of mud above
ground.   How he builds this " hut," " cone," or " turret," as it is variously called, we do not know, but it is
often two inches in height, and he keeps himself in the
top of it.   Under ordinary circumstances our cicada
would not build a hut but remain in his burrow.

Finally there comes a fateful evening when, as soon as
the sun has set, he claws his way through the top of his
mud turret or out of his burrow and looks about him
for further means of gratifying his ambitions to climb.
A bush, a tree, the highest thing within his range of vision, attracts his attention, and he hurries toward it.   It
may be he finds himself in company with many of his

kind, hurrying toward the same goal, but they are of no interest to him as yet. Like the youth in the famous poem, " Excelsior " is his motto, and he heeds no invitation to tarry. When he reaches the highest place within his ken he places himself, probably back downward, on some branch or twig and takes a firm hold with all of his six pairs of claws and keeps very still for a time. Then his skeleton nymph-skin breaks open at the back, and there pushes out of it a strange creature, long and white, except for two black spots upon his back ; on he comes until only the tip of his body remains in the old nymph-skin ; then he reaches forward and grasps the twig with his soft, new legs and pulls himself entirely clear from the old hermit garb. At once his wings begin to grow ; at first they are mere pads on his back, but they soon expand until they cover his body and are flat like those of a miller. The many veins in the wings are white, and he keeps the wings fluttering in order that they may harden soon. If, in the moonlight of some June evening, a junior naturalist should see a tree covered with cicadas at this stage, he would think it had suddenly blossomed into beautiful, white, fluttering flowers.

As the night wears on, the color of our hero changes and his wings harden, until when the sun rises we behold him in the glory of a black uniform, with facings of orange and with beautiful glassy wings folded roof-like above his body (Fig. 47). Great is the change wrought in his appearance during this one momentous night, and greater still the change wrought in his habits! Good-by now to cowl and robe. The gay knight in armor that wore them has thrown them aside

and left them clinging like a ghost of a hermit to the spot where they were abandoned.

The knight is not alone; there are thousands of his kind about him — a fact which he realizes with great joy. So happy is he that he feels as if he must burst

Fig. 47. "Good-by now to cowl and robe."

if he does not find some adequate means for expressing his happiness in this beautiful world of sunshine. Then suddenly he finds in himself the means of expression and bursts into song. Yet, it is not a song exactly, for he is a drummer rather than a singer. On his body, just behind each of his hind wings, is a kettledrum. The head to this drum is of parchment thrown into folds and may be seen with a lens if you lift his wings and look closely. Instead of drumsticks he uses a pair of strong muscles to throw the membranes

into vibration, and there is a complex arrangement of
cavities and sounding-boards around these drum-heads,
so that the noise he gives off is a great one indeed for
a fellow of his size. So fond is he of making music
that he has no time to eat or to do aught else but to
sound rolls all the sunshiny day. He is not the
only musician on the tree; there are many others, and
they all join in a swelling chorus that has been described
as a roar like that made by the "rushing of a strong
wind through the trees."

If our cicada could talk to one of you junior naturalists he would tell you that there was a good reason
for all this music. He would explain that only the
men of the cicada world possess drums, and that the
object and reason of all their music was the entertainment of the lady cicadas, who are not only very fond
of this drumming but are good critics of cicada music
as well. He would perhaps tell you also that he had
his eye on a certain graceful maiden perched on the
leaf between him and the sun; but she, on the other
hand, seemed to give about equal attention to him and
three other drummers situated near by. Excited by the
competition and by her indifference he rattled his drum
faster and faster until he arose to the heights of cicada
melody and harmony that left his rivals far behind.
Then the lady of his choice listened spellbound and

pronounced him the greatest of all musicians, and thus he won his bride. However, we may safely predict that their wedded life will be too full of happiness to last. After a few weeks the sunshine, the music, the happiness of wooing and winning will prove too much for our hero, and one day he will beat his drum in a last mad ecstasy and fall to earth and die from happy exhaustion. His little wife may survive him only long enough to cut some slits in some of the twigs of the home tree and place in them rows of eggs from which shall develop a family of hermits which shall come forth and fill the world with their music seventeen years hence, when our junior naturalists are men and women grown.

There are many broods of the cicadas in the United States, so that they appear in different localities in different years. New York State has five well-marked broods : one in the western counties is due in 1917 ; a large brood on Long Island and near Rochester will appear in 1919 ; another on Long Island in 1906 ; another in the Hudson River Valley in 1911. The different appearances of some of these broods have been noted and studied for more than a century.

Thus we know that these little hermit brothers belong to one of America's most ancient races. It will always be interesting for any junior naturalist

who has the opportunity to witness the issuing of one
of these broods to count back and find how few generations of them have passed since only Indians listened
when they came forth from their caves and beat out
their last brief days in happy cicadan minstrelsy.

INDEX

Akers, Elizabeth, 13, 16, 19.
Amazons, 79, 82, 83.
Anacreon, 12.
Ants, 59–94.
  Agricultural, 86.
  Honey, 72.
  Leaf-cutter, 72, 76.
  White, 56, 61, 71, 78.
Aphids, 76, 77, 126.
Aphis-lion, 126–130.

Basswood, 37, 38.
Basswood Leaf-roller, 119–124.
Battles, 79, 83, 84.
Bees, 4, 9, 55–94.
  Carpenter, Little, 108–117.
Beetles, 4.
Bryant, Wm. C., 7, 9.
Butterflies, 4, 30, 39–54.
Byron, Lord, 13.

Caddice-fly, 133–138.
Caddice-worm, 133–138.
Carolina Locust, 15.
Cement Maker, 97–101.
Ceratina dupla, 108–117.
Chrysopa, 125–131.
Cicada, 4, 10, 12, 13.
  septendecem, 140–149.
  tibicen, 10–12.
Communal Habitations, 53, 63, 81, 84–88.
  Wealth, 73.
Corn-root Plant-louse, 77.

Cows, Ant's, 76, 77.
Cricket, 4, 20–27.

Danaus plexippus, 48–54.
Dissosteira Carolina, 15.
Division of Labor, 57, 66, 72.
Dog-day Harvest-fly, 10–12.
Dragonflies, 4.
Drones, 62, 64.
Drummers, 11, 12, 14, 146.
Dweller in Tents, A, 119.

Ears, Insect's, 2, 16, 20, 24.
Elder, 108.
Elm, 139, 141.
Emerson, Ralph Waldo, 10.
Eumenes fraterna, 101–106.

Fabre, J.-H., 103.
Fiddlers, 14, 27.
Fireflies, 4.
Fitch, Dr. Asa, 35.
Flies, 4–7.
Fungi, 72.

Golden-eyes, 125–131.
Grandfather Graybeard, 29.
Grasshoppers, 4, 14–17.

Hermit and Troubadour, 140.
Holmes, Oliver Wendell, 18.
Homer, 12.
Hunt, Leigh, 14, 21.
Hydropsyche, 133–138.

Hymenoptera, 4, 9, 10, 55–94, 96–117.

Ichneumon, 115, 116.
Identity of Interests, 88.
Individualism, as taught by the Bees, 92.
Insect Music, 3–27, 146.

Jug Builder, The, 101–106.

Katydid, 4, 18–20.
Keats, John, 14.

Lace-wing Fly, 125–131.
Limenitis archippus, 39–54.
Lintner, Dr. J. A., 35.
Little Carpenter Bee, 108–117.
Love-singers, 10–27.
Lyreman, The, 10–13.

Maple Leaf-cutter, 30–38.
Mayer, Prof. A. M., 8.
Military Forces, 78.
Milkweed, 49.
Minnesingers, 10.
Monarch Butterfly, 48–54.
Mosquito, 7, 8.
Moths, 4, 32, 35, 124, 137.
Mud Dauber, 97–101.
Musical Organs, Flies and Bees, 6; Cicada, 11, 146; Grasshopper, 14–18; Katydid, 20; Cricket, 22.

Nomad, A Little, 29.

Orchestra, Insect, 26, 27.
Orthoptera, 14–26.

Pantographa limata, 119–124.
Paraclemensia acerifoliella, 29–38.
Pipers, The, 6.
Plant-lice, 76, 77, 126.

Poplar, 41.
Pyralidina, 124.

Queen Ants, 61.
Bee, 6, 57–61.

Raspberry, 108.
Riley, James Whitcomb, 15, 18.

Sanitation, 90.
Sceliphron caementarius, 97–101.
Scudder, Dr. S. H., 39.
Seine Maker, A, 133.
Seventeen-year Locust, 140–149.
Sheep in Wolf's Clothing, A, 39.
Slavery, 78–82.
Snowy Tree-cricket, 24–27.
Socialism, The Perfect, 55.
Soldiers, 78, 79.
Spiders, 99, 100.
Squirrel, 30.
Story we love Best, The, 108.
Sumac, 108, 111.

Tactful Mother, A, 125.
Tennyson, Alfred, 6.
Termites, 56, 61, 71, 78.
Thread-waisted Wasps, 96, 97.
Tiger Swallowtail, 30.
Tortricina, 124.
Two Mother Masons, 96.

Viceroy Butterfly, 39–49, 53.
Virgil, 13.

War, 78, 83.
Wasps, 56, 73, 81, 85, 96–106, 114.
Water Sprite, 133.
White Ants, 56, 61, 71, 78.
Willow, 41.
Workers, 66.

Xenarchus, 13.

Library of Congress Cataloging in Publication Data
(For library cataloging purposes only)

Comstock, Anna Botsford, 1854–1930.
  Ways of the six-footed.

  Reprint of the ed. published by Ginn, Boston.
  Includes index.
  1. Insects.   I. Title.
QL467.C73   1977   595.7   76-56639
ISBN 0-8014-1081-9